The Holy Eucharist

THE OSCOTT SERIES

General Editors
+ Maurice Couve de Murville, Archbishop of Birmingham
Fr David McLoughlin
Fr David Evans

Oscott College was founded near Birmingham in 1794 at a time when students and staff from the English Catholic colleges abroad were being driven home by the French Revolution. In 1838 it occupied new buildings at Sutton Coldfield, built in the Gothic style, in a move which inaugurated an ambitious phase of the Catholic Revival in England. Oscott is the seminary of the Archdiocese of Birmingham which also has students from many other dioceses.

The **Oscott Series** aims at continuing the role of Oscott as an intellectual and spiritual centre of English Catholicism for clos eon two hundred years.

Other titles in the series are:

1. **The Unsealed Fountain:**
   Essays on the Christian Spiritual Tradition
   + Maurice Couve de Murville (ed.)

2. **Niels Stensen:**
   Scientist and Saint
   Erik Kennet Pålsson

3. **Secret Hiding Places**
   Michael Hodgetts

4. **Reapers of the Harvest:**
   The Redemptorists in Great Britain and Ireland 1843–1898

5. **Holy Order**
   The Apostolic Ministry from The New Testament to the Second Vatican Council
   Aidan Nichols

Aidan Nichols OP

The Holy Eucharist

From the New Testament to Pope John Paul II

Oscott 6

VERITAS

First published 1991 by
Veritas Publications
7–8 Lower Abbey Street
Dublin 1

Copyright © Aidan Nichols OP 1991

ISBN 1 85390 182 2

Cover design by Banahan McManus
Typesetting by Computertype, Dublin
Printed in the Republic of Ireland by The Leinster Leader

Contents

Preface   7

Chapter 1   The Eucharist in the New Testament   9
Chapter 2   The Eucharist in the Age of the Fathers   34
Chapter 3   The Mediaevals on the Nature of the
             Real Presence   58
Chapter 4   The Mediaevals on the Purpose of the
             Real Presence   76
Chapter 5   The Eucharistic Sacrifice from Trent to
             the Nineteenth Century   87
Chapter 6   Catholic Eucharistic Theology in the
             Twentieth Century   102
Chapter 7   A Systematic Summary: Balthasar and
             John Paul II   120

Appendix: The Eucharist in Anglicanism   125

Notes   133

Bibliography   148

Index of Names   151

Preface

Another book on the Eucharist? My excuse must be that
its approach is, in current English-speaking Catholic
theology, sufficiently distinctive, in that it gives due weight
to each principal period in the development of the Church's
eucharistic doctrine, neither treating modern theology as the
'one thing necessary' nor writing it off as thin gruel, compared
with the more nourishing fare of the dogmatic tradition.
As with my earlier book, *Holy Order* (to which *The Holy
Eucharist* is designed as a complement), doctrinal development
is treated as a homogeneous process, not a series of
disconnected starts. The historic theologies of the Church
— from the inspired ones of the New Testament, through
the Fathers and mediaeval divines to the early modern and
modern periods — are regarded as presupposing and building
on one another in the many-roomed mansion of the Church,
not as sparks flying off from some ecclesiastical catherine
wheel to lose themselves in a lonely extinction in the heavens.

As with *Holy Order*, if more briefly, I take a contemporary
text of the magisterium as providing a convenient synthesis
of earlier doctrine. In the previous book, this was a document
of the Second Vatican Council. Here it is a letter of Pope
John Paul II (hence my sub-title) preceded by a scattering
of references to the great contemporary 'Church Father',
Hans Urs von Balthasar, whom that pope has sought to
make a theological light to irradiate the present-day Church.
If the resultant 'systematic summary' is short, this is not
least because the complexity of eucharistic theology can,
as *The Holy Eucharist* suggests, be captured in three themes:
the Eucharist as presence, as sacrifice, and as the Church's
foundation. The reader may wonder why a fourth theme
of specifically eucharistic theology, the Eucharist as
anticipation of the banquet of the Kingdom, has not been
made a structuring principle in the making of this book.
Dear to modern Eastern Orthodox theology in particular,

and stressed by a variety of modern western authors, both Protestant and Catholic, that theme has notably influenced the revision of the Roman rite (especially the new Eucharistic Prayers) and the liturgies of separated Western ecclesial communities — although in practice the secularisation of the historic Christianity of the West is more evident than its 're-eschatologisation'. That theme has not been explicitly presented here as a formal principle of selection for the materials offered, since it is, in my view, so pervasively implicit in the other three. For if the Eucharist is the real presence of Christ — *autobasileia*, 'the Kingdom in person', as Origen of Alexandria called him — and if, also, its offering is one with that heavenly Sacrifice which, for St John in his Apocalypse, is the central reality of the New Jerusalem, the City of the End; and if, finally, its celebration lies at the foundation of the Church, herself the 'sacrament of the Kingdom', as the Second Vatican Council puts it, then how can the Holy Eucharist *not* be the icon, and the foretaste, of the feast of the Kingdom, when we shall be, in full reality, God's people, and he, in truth, our God.

Aidan Nichols OP
Blackfriars
Cambridge
Memorial day of
St Bonaventure 1991

1

The Eucharist in the New Testament

The plan of this study could be called 'genetic', for it begins from the *genesis* of the Eucharist, and the Christian understanding thereof, in the New Testament. Having then looked at those glorious beginnings, we shall be in a good position to trace the development of eucharistic doctrine up to the modern period. A brief, systematic account of the Eucharist, based on some twentieth century theologies, will provide an obvious *finale*.

The Gospel of John

I shall begin with the Eucharist as portrayed in the Gospel according to St John, since this is the gospel where the Eucharist is first promised by Jesus. By way of preface, it seem appropriate to touch on the general issue of St John's Gospel and 'sacramentalism' — a view of faith intimately bound up with sacraments, with belief in their dominical origin, with their celebration and with the divine life which flows from them. Many exegetes see a rich range of sacramental references scattered through this gospel. They detect symbolic references to Baptism in Johannine passages mentioning water. And they find similar allusions to the Eucharist in passages dealing with meals, with crucial components of those meals — bread and wine, and with the natural provenance of wine, namely the vine. These students include such non-Catholic scholars as, in Switzerland, the Lutheran Oscar Cullmann, and, in England, the Congregationalist C. K. Barrett, though it is Catholic exegetes who have argued for the broadest range of sacramental reference, extending to Matrimony at Cana and even the Anointing of the Sick in the scene of anointing Jesus' feet at Bethany.[1]

Almost all of these proposed sacramental references work, as already indicated, by means of *symbolism*. Early Christians, so the argument runs, owing to their conviction that the prophecies of the Old Testament had found their fulfilment in Christ, were acutely sensitive to symbolism, or, more precisely, to typology — the idea that one event may stand as the fulfilment, whether partial or complete, of another. Given this backcloth of habitual perception, it was entirely reasonable for John to present Jesus' words and actions as prophetic types of the sacraments of the Church — rather than presenting the sacraments directly, as in the other gospels. St John does not, for instance, describe the institution of the Eucharist at the Last Supper, nor does he record the command to baptise found in Matthew 28. It was to those omissions that the exegetical school of the 'existentialist' Lutheran Rudolf Bultmann looked for support in their contention that John is a non-sacramental — or even an anti-sacramental — author. They maintain, or maintained, that where sacramental references in his gospel can scarcely be denied, so manifest are they, they should be ascribed, none the less, to the interventions of an otherwise altogether unknown figure, the 'ecclesiastical redactor'.[2] But, as Father Raymond Brown has pointed out in his great commentary, *The Gospel according to John*, the fact that the fourth evangelist does not associate the sacraments with one single, all-important saying of Jesus, uttered at the end of his life and forming part of his final instructions to the disciples, by no means entails that St John is uninterested in the sacraments. On the contrary, the scattering of such references through the historic ministry may imply that John had a stronger, not weaker, sacramental sense than his fellows.[3] For his gospel, the sacraments, as the Church's principal institutions, are rooted in much, or even everything, that Jesus said and did.

The promise of the institution of the Eucharist is found in St John's sixth chapter. That chapter opens with the miracle of the multiplication of the loaves and fishes, a parallel to the Feeding of the Five Thousand in the Synoptic tradition. John describes Jesus' actions in terms of the three principal verbs of the Synoptic institution narrative: Jesus took; he gave thanks, and he distributed. Unlike the Synoptics, John has our Lord doing the actual distribution of the multiplied loaves, looking forward, perhaps, to the moment of the Supper. Moreover, whereas the Synoptics report that large quantities of both bread and fish remained after the miracle, John mentions only bread. He was already thinking, probably, of the 'imperishable bread' which Jesus will soon be speaking about. Finally, John's remark that the miracle took place 'shortly before the Jewish feast of Passover' seems gratuitous unless he wanted his readers to make the mental connection with the Eucharist, instituted as that was at the last Passover of the Lord's life.

For all these reasons, we are justified in hearing, in this event, eucharistic undertones. Bread is multiplied to feed a crowd; at the Last Supper Jesus will use bread to bring about a related miracle, feeding many spiritually with himself. The bread of the multiplication is offered to all those following Jesus; similarly, the sacrament will be at the disposition of all believers. The bread satisfies those who eat, and some is left over; just so, communion will nourish disciples, and in a way which is infinite or inexhaustible.[4] Not surprisingly, therefore, this passage is drawn on by the Eucharistic Prayer found in the primitive Christian document called the *Didache,* 'teaching' (of the apostles).

> We give thanks to you, our Father. ... As this fragmented bread was scattered on the mountains, but was gathered up and became one, so let the Church be gathered up from the four corners of the earth into your Kingdom.[5]

Interestingly, John records that the multiplication took place on a mountain, and that the crowds assembled there acclaimed Jesus as, precisely, a king.[6]

After the multiplication episode comes John's version of

11

Jesus' walking on the Sea of Galilee. For some commentators, this too is eucharistic in John's eyes. Jesus arrives at the boat containing Peter and the others in a quasi-instantaneous way, as though, for him, space hardly exists. Analogously, in the Eucharist we find the difference between our space and time and that of the ascended body of our Lord is taken away. The comparison may be thought a little strained. Still, the walking on the water brings home to John's readers the fact that in Jesus God's omnipotence is at work. Jesus masters the elements of nature, and identifies himself with the words 'It is I', perhaps a form of the divine Name, *ego eimi,* 'I am'. And, of course, only omnipotent divinity could give to an ordinary element like bread the qualities which Jesus will later ascribe to it.

And so we come to the discourse on the Bread of Life itself, usually reckoned as constituted by this chapter's verses 22 to 59 inclusive. The connection of the discourse with the multiplication incident is not simply in the realm of symbolic suggestiveness. There is also a causal link: the crowd are looking for more food (no doubt many of them lived at the merest subsistence level), but Jesus counsels them to seek the 'bread of life', 'bread from heaven', a food which nourishes 'for eternal life'. Referring back to the event of the Exodus, Jesus affirms that the manna of the desert was only a type or foreshadowing of the food that he can give. Now we know from the Jewish 'pseudepigrapha', the non-canonical literature of the inter-testamental period, that Jews in Jesus' lifetime associated quite specific expectations with the manna of old. For many, the coming of the Messiah would be announced by a renewal of the miracles of the Exodus, and notably of the gift of manna. The Apocalypse of Baruch prophesies that

> the manna will come down again, and will be eaten. . .[7]

and one of the *midrashim,* a piece of early rabbinic freestyle interpreting of the Hebrew Bible, reads:

> The last liberator will act like the first. What did the

12

first liberator do? He made manna come down, as it is said, 'Behold I will rain down bread from heaven for you' (Exodus 16:14). And so the last liberator will make manna come down, as it is said, 'wheaten bread will be spread over the earth' (Psalm 72:10).[8]

But Jesus warns the Jews that the bread he is concerned with will not be just a repeat performance, on a grander scale, of the miracle of physical feeding performed for their ancestors.

> It was not Moses who gave you bread from heaven; . . . it is my Father who gives you the bread from heaven, the true bread.[9]

In the section of the discourse which follows, most commentators seem agreed that the 'bread' which the Father will thus give is here the Saviour himself — whether in his person, in his gifts at large, in his teaching, in his grace, or any selection from, or combination of, these realities. By faith, the disciple must attach himself to the Saviour's person, word and works, for Christ is the Word sent from the Father. In this way, eternal life will come about in him:

> I am the bread of life; he who comes to me will never be hungry, he who believes in me will never thirst.[10]

The language here is reminiscent of Jesus' conversation with the Samaritan woman in John 4, where the teaching and grace of the Saviour are described as water he will give, water so welling up in the recipient that he will never be thirsty again. So far, then, up to verse 48, although the Eucharist is not excluded from the terms of the discussion (for it is certainly a gift of God in Christ) it has not yet been formally introduced. In its earliest unfolding, the discourse looks not so much forwards to the sacrament as backwards to the Old Testament figure of Wisdom. Like the personified divine Wisdom, Jesus will feed human beings on his teaching. Indeed, in the Book of Proverbs, Wisdom had cried out:

> Come, eat of my bread, and drink the wine I have prepared.[11]

But in verses 48 to 51 the discourse shifts its axis. In a fresh emphasis, the speaker declares himself to be the bread of life which must actually be eaten, the word 'eat' recurring four times in a relatively small number of verses. As has often been observed, were Jesus not moving on, at this juncture, to speak of a genuine eating — a literal meal — then something very odd has occurred. Having expounded a christological idea in clear terms, he is repeating it in a new form not only enigmatic but also, frankly, repellent. In Semitic languages the idiom 'to eat someone's flesh' exists, but it means to injure somebody, to do them harm — rather like the contemporary English slang expression 'to bite someone's head off'. And as for the drinking of blood, that had even more unattractive associations. The Mosaic Law rigorously forbade the consuming of blood, even of animal blood. Not surprisingly, therefore, Jesus' hearers lodge a protest. 'How can this man give us his flesh to eat?' Perhaps they misunderstood. Yet on all occasions in the Gospel when Jesus' audience objects through some lack of comprehension, Jesus immediately makes it clear that they have presumed a misplaced literalness: he was only speaking figuratively. A good instance can be found in John 4:

> He said, 'I have food to eat that you do not know about'. So the disciples asked one another, 'Has someone been bringing him food?' But Jesus said, 'My "food" is to do the will of the One who sent me and to complete his work'.[12]

On the other hand, when the Lord's teaching has been correctly understood yet found objectionable, it is typical of him to re-state it without in any way softening its force. And so in John 8 Jesus addresses his Jewish opponents:

> 'Your father Abraham rejoiced to think that he would see my Day; he saw it and was glad'. The Jews then

said, 'You are not fifty yet, and you have seen Abraham?' Jesus replied, 'I tell you most solemnly, before Abraham was, I am'.[13]

It is the second kind of response which we find in the discourse on the Bread of Life. Jesus insists, 'My flesh is real food, my blood is real drink': a reiteration which must count as the doctrine of the real presence in its Johannine form.

This flesh-food, blood-drink leads to the mutual indwelling or 'abiding', *menein*, of Christ and the believer. From this eating and drinking the latter will draw everlasting life. Jesus goes on to ask the disciples:

> Does this scandalise you? What if you should see the Son of Man ascending to where he was before?[14]

The miracle of the Ascension (not described separately from the Resurrection in this Gospel) will demonstrate the power of the Saviour, while his return to the Father will, thanks to the 'Paraclete', the Holy Spirit, make it possible for the disciples to encounter his glorified humanity in a new way.

But then Jesus adds the comment much exploited since by controversialists hostile to the doctrine of the eucharistic presence:

> It is the spirit that gives life; the flesh has nothing to offer.[15]

Yet the Fourth Gospel, which, in its prologue, proclaims itself the Gospel of the Logos incarnate, cannot write off the flesh as irrelevant to the economy of salvation — or, at least, it cannot do that without falling into self-contradiction. If, then, we look for an interpretation of this saying consistent with the evangelist's wider message, we find two candidates. For the first, Jesus is stressing that the unique food and drink he promises are not to be valued because they are flesh or inasmuch as they are flesh. The 'flesh', the bodily presence, is of value in so far as it carries the life of God. It is valuable as the mode in which the

Logos is present to the world from the moment of the Incarnation onwards. For an alternative reading, the ground of the contrast between flesh and spirit does not lie in the difference between two aspects of Jesus' reality as the Word made flesh, but between two ways of approaching his teaching. On this view, 'flesh', purely human understanding, cannot grasp the meaning of his words. His teaching is divine, and to be appropriated by us requires the help of the Father. Jesus' altercation with the Pharisees in John 8:14-15 turns on this distinction. The Pharisees judge 'according to the flesh', by merely human standards, whereas Jesus judges soundly since, as he remarks:

I am not alone: the One who sent me is with me.

Finally, the discourse on the Bread of Life closes with a reference to Judas Iscariot as the man who will betray the Lord — and some exegetes see in this circumstance a pointer onwards towards the Last Supper when Judas will in fact defect.

Why then does not St John proceed to describe how Jesus fulfilled his promise of the Eucharist by recounting its institution at the Last Supper just as we find in Mark, Matthew and Luke? A possible explanation derives from the purpose of the Gospel as stated by the author himself at the end of chapter 20. If the evangelist wrote (as he implies) simply in order to persuade people that 'Jesus is the Christ, the Son of God', an account of the institution of the Eucharist could not strictly be demanded from him. On the other hand, few modern students take these words of John at their face value. Those who do most commonly argue that the Fourth Gospel was intended as a handbook for missionaries in the Jewish Diaspora — the Jewish communities outside Palestine. Clearly, only Jews would be deeply concerned as to whether or not Jesus was the 'Christ', the Jewish Messiah. But other scholars maintain that, while this is indeed *one* major aim of the evangelist, and perhaps his chief aim, it is not his only one. Other goals he took in writing were, negatively, the refutation of Christian heretics and, positively, encouragement for main-line believers. And these purposes might well have been served by some account of the events of the Supper.

A second possible explanation for the absence of an institution narrative in John is that, by the time the Fourth Gospel was edited or published (perhaps soon after the year 90), the Eucharist and its founding would be so well-known that a reminder of its mere existence would be unnecessary. What was needed was, rather, a deeper grasp of the Eucharist's nature and purpose, and this John provides in chapter 6.

Thirdly, it is possible to hold that John *does* offer us an account of the Eucharist's institution during the Last Supper: in allegorical form, at the foot-washing scene of chapter 13. According to this thesis, first proposed, it would seem, by the Modernist scholar Alfred Loisy in his *Le quatrième Évangile*, the foot-washing's true theme is the Eucharist. The drama enacted by Jesus with the Twelve tells us that the Eucharist is so essential an act of the Christian life that without it one can have no share in Christ. This hypothesis is by no means fanciful. Certain features of the foot-washing do recall the Eucharist. To begin with, the cue for the foot-washing is Jesus' final break with Judas, and here we may wish to compare the Lord's offer of bread to Judas, whereupon Satan enters him, with Paul's warning to the Corinthian Christians about the communicant who eats and drinks 'to his own condemnation'.[17] Again, the commandment of love which Jesus issues at the foot-washing sounds remarkably akin to the principle of agape, or mutual charity, associated with the eucharistic feast. And most important of all, the 'High-Priestly Discourse' of Jesus which follows on the foot-washing also appears to possess definitely eucharistic resonances.

> I consecrate myself for them that they may be consecrated in the truth.

Loisy paraphrased these words as:

I vow myself to die as an expiatory victim, so that the blood of Calvary and the Eucharist may purify them of their sins.[18]

This whole section of the Fourth Gospel has been quarried by later liturgical compilers, intent on collecting suitable formulae for the Eucharistic Prayers. At the very least, the words of Jesus as given here are much more appropriate if Jesus did institute the Eucharist at this moment. The foot-washing, then, may well represent not only the unique act of service which Christ performed by his atoning death but also the permanent efficacious memorial of that act of service, the Eucharist.[19]

The Johannine passion narrative does not finish without a further, final eucharistic reference when the eye-witness reports on the blood and water which flowed from the Lord's riven side on the Cross.[20] This flux of bloody water serves firstly as a certification that Jesus is truly dead, but its significance transcends the simply physiological. By this point in the Gospel, water and blood are well-established as signs of salvation. The soldier's lance-thrust demonstrates, certainly, the reality of Jesus' death, but this death, paradoxically, is the beginning of new life. From the corpse of the Saviour there flows the living water which will be, as he predicted, a source of life for all who believe in him.[21] Suitably, the opening of Jesus' side recalls the insistence of the Jewish law of sacrifice that the priest should split the heart of the victim, and make the blood come forth.[22] So Jesus dies a sacrificial victim. To which we may add that John probably expected his readers to think more specifically here of the sacraments of Baptism and the Eucharist which mediate the new life in Christ.

It remains to inquire what part the Eucharist plays in St John's overall presentation of the Gospel. For such a many-faceted jewel of a text, no one angle of vision will suffice, but we may attempt an answer to our question by taking up three complementary perspectives. First, the importance of the Eucharist in Johannine teaching can be expressed in terms of the motif of eternal life. In the Fourth Gospel, the Word is made flesh so as to become not only the way and the truth but also the life. Through the waters of Baptism, and the Holy Spirit, he gives human beings a new birth. By the food and drink of the Eucharist, and the consequent gift of his own person, he nurtures and develops this new, supernatural life. Secondly, the role of the Eucharist in John can be put in terms of spiritual relationship. The Word comes to unite God to humanity by the mutual indwelling of Jesus and his brethren. This reciprocal abiding is initiated by the divine gifts of faith and love, and — as the inevitable consequence of loving the Jesus who is thus believed in — by the observance of his commandments. But a more intimate, and more intensely real, form of this same relationship is achieved through the Eucharist. Lastly, the place of the Eucharist in the Gospel of John can be located not so much, this time, by reference to the Incarnation (as in the two schemata outlined so far), but in connection with the Atonement. On Calvary, Jesus gives up his bodily existence for the life of the world, so as to bestow resurrection and the life everlasting. But this death does not conclude his own role in the work of salvation. By his death, the incarnate Word creates the basis for his offer of the gift of salvation, an offer claimed by us in Baptism ('water') and actually received in eucharistic communion ('blood'). The Eucharist is the supreme means initiated by Christ for the communication of 'eternal life' — itself the Johannine version of the 'reign' or 'Kingdom' of God which Jesus preached.[23]

The Eucharist in the Synoptics and St Paul

Leaving aside the tacit allusiveness of the Fourth Gospel, we possess four sources for the institution of the Eucharist: Mark, Matthew, Luke and Paul. The Marcan and Matthaean accounts are very similar, while Luke's chimes more closely with Paul's. Looking first at Mark and Matthew, what did the first Christians believe happened at the Last Supper? We must note at once that these first two Synoptic evangelists present the Last Supper along the lines of a Passover meal.

The Jewish Passover was originally a spring sacrifice of lambs, held in acknowledgement of the return of life after winter. The early Israelites, following what they believed to be the revealed will of God, turned it into a thanksgiving and communion sacrifice in celebration of their miraculous escape from Egypt. Although in earlier post-Exodus times, the ritual was carried out in each household, a change came about in this respect with the Josianic or Deuteronomic reform of the seventh century before Christ. Henceforth, the actual sacrificing would be done in the Jerusalem temple, but the victim, the food, was still eaten in the family circle. During the sacred meal, the narrative of the Exodus was related in a paraphrase, the *haggadah*, and the entire order of service became known as the *seder*. The Marcan-Matthaean account of the Last Supper reproduces several constitutive features of the Passover *seder*: most importantly, the blessing, breaking and presentation of unleavened wafers or 'azymes'; the blessing and distribution of cups of wine; and the 'Hallel chant', the singing of the final verses of Psalm 118, the customary *finale* of the rite.[24] A number of details confirm the thesis that the Last Supper was the last Passover of Jesus' life: the holding of this meal at night; the disciples' reclining at table, not usual among Palestinian Jews but a ritual duty at Passover as a symbol of freedom; the drinking of wine, used in everyday life at this period for medicinal purposes only; the beginning to eat before the breaking of bread, something which only happened at Passover; the assumption on Judas' departure of a commission to do something for the poor, a pious commonplace of the Passover feast; and last but not least, the fact that Jesus, in ritually interpreting the significance of the bread and wine, gave his own personal version of the Passover *haggadah*.[25]

By omitting the sacrificial lamb, and identifying *himself* with the blessed bread and wine which were its accompaniments, Jesus presents himself as the new Passover victim to be fed on at the Supper. It coheres with this interpretation to see the breaking of bread as representing, in this case, the violence of the death of Jesus, and the pouring out of wine as standing, similarly, for the shedding of his blood. The consumption of the elements would be, then, a common sharing in the sacrificial death of the Redeemer.

Before going further into these doctrinal implications of the Marcan-Matthaean account we must, however, pause to consider a difficulty. While, as we have seen, the Gospel of St John does not offer an institution narrative except perhaps allegorically, John's version of the Passion presumes that Jesus died on Passover eve — which sets back the timing of the Last Supper to before the feast has begun. Earlier this century, most exegetes took it for granted that the Johannine dating was purely symbolic. In order to stress that, as the Baptist proclaimed, Jesus is truly the 'Lamb of God who takes away the sins of the world', the fourth evangelist allowed himself the liberty of bringing forward the date of Jesus' death by one day. While hundreds and thousands of paschal lambs were being slaughtered in the temple, the true paschal Lamb died unrecognised outside the gates of the city. More recently, scholars have rallied to the Johannine reckoning considered as chronology also. Research has increasingly vindicated John's knowledge and accuracy in matters of Jewish customs and liturgy as well as Palestinian geography. This creates the presumption that the evangelist found his symbolism already inscribed in the contours of literal reality — rather than rearranging the letters of the real to spell the theological symbols on which he had decided. Following John has the advantage of removing certain difficulties in the Synoptic account of the death of Jesus, notably the apparent conflict between the provisions of the Jewish law for what to do — or, more often, what not to do — on a high festival day, and certain elements in the Passion narrative such as the carrying of arms by the high priest's servants, the purchase of Jesus' burial shroud, and the meeting of the Sanhedrin, the Jewish governing council, during the night of the feast. The Lutheran exegete Joachim Jeremias argues that all of these elements can be justified as historically plausible; but not everyone concurs. If, however, we choose to follow the Johannine chronology, we call into question, seemingly, the paschal — that is, the Passover — character of the Last Supper. In John, the Jews refuse to accompany Jesus into Pilate's palace on the day of his arrest because

> there was the paschal meal to be eaten, and they must not incur defilement[26]

and Pilate hands Jesus over for crucifixion 'on the eve of the paschal feast'.[27] For the Fourth Gospel the Eucharist was apparently instituted on a Wednesday, the day before Passover, which began on Thursday evening. Here the paschal nature of the Last Supper is retrenched; it becomes simply a theological idea on the part of **Mark and** Matthew. Though the Last Supper was not, empirically **speaking**, a Passover meal, Mark and Matthew choose theologically to present it so. We for our part should have to defend their decision by similarly theological, not chronological, argumentation. Since Jesus has won our definitive liberation from sin and for God, the whole life of the Church is a kind of continuous Passover — a celebration of death to sin, and life to God. On this basis, Mark and Matthew could legitimately present the Supper, and so the Eucharist, as a Christian Passover.

But we are not obliged to choose between these stark alternatives, one of which regards John as unhistorical, and the other of which makes the same charge against Mark and Matthew. Two other possibilities exist. First, and quite simply, it may be that Jesus deliberately brought forward the Passover meal in anticipation of his arrest. Secondly, and this is more complex, the Jewish calendar in the time of Jesus may not have been uniform. Indeed, it is known that in some respects it was not uniform.[28] For instance, the Pharisee party disagreed with the Sadduccees about the date of the Jewish Pentecost. Moreover, the Qumran manuscripts — the 'Dead Sea Scrolls' — show that some Jews of the period rejected even the basics of the official calendar, a lunar calender introduced under Hellenistic influence not that long previously. They preferred the solar calendar found in the Book of Jubilees, a more traditionally Jewish way of dating associated with the work of the Priestly School during the Exile in Babylon. In the conservative milieux which produced the Book of Jubilees the solar calendar was itself regarded as part of the Mosaic revelation. For this older system of dating, Passover, the fifteenth day of the first month, always fell on a Wednesday, with the Passover meal eaten on Tuesday night. In view of the tension between Jesus and the Temple authorities, it may be that it pleased him to follow this alternative calendar. There is reason to think that, in various quarters of the early Church, the Lord's arrest in the course of the night that followed the Last Supper was dated, in the common memory, to a Wednesday. The *Didache* expects Christians to fast on Wednesdays, and the Syrian treatise called the *Didascalia Apostolorum*, a third-century work, attributes this to Jesus' Wednesday arrest. Writers as far apart geographically as Cyprus (Epiphanius of Salamis) and what is now Hungary (Victorinus of Petau, who lived in the ancient Pannonia) show awareness of this tradition. Among the moderns, some favour this dating on the ground that a great many events must otherwise be crowded into a very short space of time.[29] On this view, the Last Supper was celebrated at Passover 'old style', an occasion when groups that found themselves conscientiously unable to sacrifice in the Temple might immolate the offering in their own homes, reverting to the primitive practice of Exodus 12,[30] whereas Jesus actually died on Passover 'new style'. All of this is highly pertinent to the idea of the Eucharist as the Christian sacrifice. To justify the sacrificial character ascribed by Church tradition to the Eucharist, the Passover connection seems vital.

With this in mind, let us return to Mark and Matthew. Granted that the actions of Jesus at his Last Supper were borrowed from the Passover *seder*, of fundamental importance for the novel factors which Jesus added to the inherited

23

ritual are his words — what we now know as the 'words of consecration'. It is the words which provide the clue to why this Passover meal differed from all the rest.

Over the bread, Jesus says: 'This is my body', meaning 'What I show you is my body', for the phrase *touto esti* locates some feature of the environment to which the speaker would draw attention, like the Latin *ecce*, the French *voici*, the English 'behold' or a second Greek version of the same thing, also found in the gospels, *idou*. The form of words which Jesus elects is reminiscent of a passage about the institution of the Sinai covenant in the book of Exodus: 'Behold the blood of the covenant'; 'This is the blood of the covenant that the Lord has made with you'. The phrase *touto esti*, translates word for word as the familiar 'this is', and a major issue which the words of institution raise concerns the degree of force claimed by the Greek verb 'to be', *einai*, in this context. When Jesus uses this phrase to pick out the bread of the Supper and calls it 'my body', is he declaring it to be identical with his body, as the developed faith of Catholic Christianity would suggest? Or, rather, is he simply saying that it will symbolise or represent his body? (The same problem arises, evidently, in connection with the wine of the Supper and his blood.) *Au fond*, is this an act of identification, or one of symbolisation? Is Jesus, by his power as the mediator between God and humanity, personally united as he is (for the christological faith of the Seven Councils) to the Lord of Israel, the Creator, as well as a human being like ourselves, in the process of rendering the bread one reality with himself, or is he in the course of creating a symbolic object which will 'stand for' himself in the Community of his disciples?

The theory of symbolism, unfortunately, is nowadays an extremely complex and somewhat confusing area of thought, with cross-connections to and from such disciplines as semantics (the theory of language) and hermeneutics (the theory of interpretation) as well as aesthetics, psychology and (cultural) anthropology. That theory, at least where linguistic symbols are concerned, has even generated a discipline of its own: 'semiotics', the theory of signs, from the Greek *sêmeion*. To survive in this jungle, we must hack our way through a huge amount of scholarly undergrowth. Fundamentally, it may be said, there are three categories of symbolic object.[31] The first houses objects that are naturally symbolic — not in the sense that an object occurring in nature may strike us as expressive of something beyond itself, but in the sense of something fashioned deliberately, by human intention, for the serving of some symbolic end. Thus, if I visit an art gallery and overhear the guide pointing to a Greek figurine with the words 'This is Plato', I rightly conclude that he or she means, This is an image of Plato. Secondly, there are objects which are not symbolic by nature yet become so through usage or convention. Thus a piece of cloth woven from red, white and blue threads is not naturally symbolic, but by a convention indicated in calling it a 'tricouleur', it becomes symbolic as a representation of France. Thirdly, there may also be objects which are neither naturally symbolic nor symbolic through a common convention but which a given individual renders symbolic, announcing at the same time his intention of doing so. Thus Jesus, in recounting the parable of the sower, ends up by saying, 'The field is the world, the seed is the Word of God...'. We can call these 'encoded', as distinct from 'natural' and 'conventional' symbols.

None of these three types of symbolisation seem easily applicable, however, to the Marcan-Matthaean account of the Supper. Consecrated bread and wine are neither symbolic of Christ's body and blood by nature, or by common convention, nor are they related to a code in some situation where, explicitly or tacitly, Jesus announces his creation of symbols the better to convey a spiritual message. The point may be made more persuasively if we look for a moment at the possible parallels elsewhere in Scripture, investigated by those who, in Church history, have felt unable to accept an outright identification of the consecrated elements with the personal reality of Jesus Christ. In the first place, Scripture uses the verb 'to be' after a fashion cognate with the 'is' of the words of institution when it deals with the decoding of an allegory. In Daniel 7:24 for example, the prophet, invited to interpret King Belshazzar's dream, says, 'The horns are ten kingdoms', meaning, obviously, that they 'stand for' those kingdoms. But decoding an allegorical dream is an enterprise so far removed from the events of the Last Supper that it is difficult to suppose this parallel very enlightening. A second sort of possible parallel consists in what we can call the 'implicit parable'. On occasion Jesus tells parables without warning his listeners beforehand, 'Hear this parable'. An example occurs in John 15, where Jesus declares 'I am the true Vine'. Yet an explanation following hard on this statement warns hearer or reader that the affirmation is essentially symbol. He and his disciples will share one single life of mutual indwelling, just as a vine and its branches form one organic life. In other words, Jesus implicitly presents this 'is-statement' as parabolic, just as, in such Synoptic material as the story of the seed falling on different types of ground, he explicitly presents his teaching in parabolic form. Finally, we find a third sort of possible parallel: the case of the 'efficacious sign'. In Genesis 17:10, when describing the institution of circumcision in the time of the patriarchs, the biblical writer portrays God as saying, 'This (namely, circumcision) is my covenant between me and you': an efficacious means for realising the covenant with Abraham, but one which operates within the order of symbols. As we read a verse or so later, 'This will be the sign of the covenant between you and me'. Here we move much closer to the realities involved in the Last Supper — except in one major respect. What the sign of circumcision is to realise efficaciously will be a new relation of Abraham and his descendants to God; what the bread and wine of the Supper are to realise efficaciously, by contrast, is simply the person of Jesus himself, in his sacrificial dying: 'my body', 'my blood'. In so far as the consecrated elements of the Supper are, like circumcision, efficacious signs, they are signs of the presence of a person — and this amounts to saying that they are not simply symbols but are self-identically that same person, though his personhood is presented there in the order which signs inhabit. As we shall see, finding the right way to affirm that the eucharistic bread and wine are fundamentally identical with the person of Jesus, but in such a way that they remain within the order of signs has been a frequent concern in the doctrinal tradition of (in particular) the Latin Church. We shall see later, while looking at the eucharistic doctrine of the Fathers and the mediaeval divines, that calling the relationship between the elements and the divine-human victim 'symbolisation' *can* be given an acceptable meaning — so long as symbolisation is not defined over against identification, something which, for contemporary culture and consciousness in the West is, however, virtually inevitable.

Jesus' identification of his body with the paschal bread is echoed in part two of the institution narrative, the words spoken over the cup. 'This is my blood, the blood of the covenant': here there is a reference to the description, in Exodus 24, of the making of the covenant of Sinai. Evidently, Jesus is involved in establishing a covenant 'in his blood', which means: in and through his dying. Although neither Mark nor Matthew so remarks in explicit fashion, this will be a new covenant, as foretold by Jeremiah in chapter 31 of the book of his name, a prophecy much in the minds of Jesus' contemporaries, as we know from some of the Essene writings, and notably the 'Damascus Document'. Luke and Paul will be more forthright in calling this a new covenant, superseding, then, the covenant of Sinai. But if the sacrifice instituted at the Supper is to be a new version of the sacrifice given on Sinai, then it will be, like its predecessor, a sacrifice both of thanksgiving and communion. On Sinai, Moses offered bulls as a thanksgiving sacrifice, pouring half of the blood onto the altar, and sprinkling the people with the remainder, saying, 'This is the blood of the covenant': that covenant which now bound them in a closer way to the God of the Fathers. Jesus will pour out his blood on the Cross, and communicate it to the disciples so that henceforth they may be united with him. Remarkably, however, the Lord describes his blood as being poured out *now*, for he uses a present participle of the verb *ekchunnein*. So these words and actions of Jesus constitute a mysterious anticipation of the sacrifice of the Friday. That sacrifice is already present in a hidden way in the gifts of the Supper.

Nor will the scope of the new eucharistic sacrifice be confined — if that is the word! — to thanksgiving and communion. As in the developed sacrificial system of Jewish worship, it will also act as a sacrifice of atonement or expiation. As Matthew records, it is celebrated 'for the taking away of sins'.[32]

Lastly, Jesus adds the comment that he will not drink again of the fruit of the vine until the day that he drinks it anew in the kingdom of his Father. These words are generally taken to indicate an eschatological dimension to the Eucharist — some reference to the final state of humanity with God in the Age to Come. The Passover was itself a looking forward to the coming deliverance of which the escape from Egypt was the prototype. 'In that night they were redeemed, and in that night they will be redeemed'; for popular expectation, the Messiah would come on the night of the Passover.[33] Here the hope of Israel is both ratified and strengthened: the consecrated bread and wine are a pledge of the future face-to-face encounter of God and humanity, the first-fruits of the good things prepared for the disciples in the coming Kingdom.

Can we summarise, then, the contribution of the Marcan-Matthaean institution narrative to our understanding of the Eucharist? In the course of a final meal with his disciples, in a Passover celebration which he transforms by a unique gesture all his own, Jesus gave his disciples his body as their food in the form of bread, and his blood as their refreshment in the form of wine. He announced his imminent self-offering and its redemptive value. He set up a covenant between him and them, one not to be succeeded by any other before the banquet of the Kingdom at the end of time. This covenant, like that of Sinai, has its own thanksgiving and communion sacrifice, which is also a sacrifice of atonement or expiation — the Eucharist. That sacrifice, whose victim the disciples will feed on in a meal, is the pledge of the perfect union of God with humanity in the fullness of the Age to Come.

Moving on, then, to Saint Paul: the materials for his understanding of the Eucharist can be consulted in the First Letter to the Church at Corinth — a missive written from Ephesus around the year 56 — in its tenth and eleventh chapters. Paul's discussion of the Eucharist is prompted by an exhortation to the Corinthian Christians to avoid participating in anything connected with idolatrous pagan worship. Since they participate in the Christian Eucharist, they should take care not to associate themselves in any way with pagan cultus. The fortuitous arisal of the topic of the Eucharist in Paul's correspondence may bring home to us, incidentally, the occasional character of what the New Testament has to say about it. Happily, the New Testament has teaching to offer us on the Eucharist, yet as the Council of Trent implicitly points out in its teaching on Tradition, something like the Eucharist — an essential part of the Church's faith — might just have come down to us through the Church's common life and not through any writings at all. Anyhow, advising the Corinthians to steer clear of pagan celebrations, Paul asks rhetorically, 'The cup of blessing that we bless, is it not a communion in the blood of Christ?'[34] Why does he thus mention the eucharistic chalice first? Some scholars find the reason in the more perspicuous parallel between the eucharistic wine and pagan libations, which were usually themselves wine-offerings. The analogy with pagan worship would be much less obvious if Paul began by comparing the eucharistic bread to eating the meat of pagan sacrifice. Other commentators suggest that Paul wished to refer briefly to the chalice before going on to reflect in a more developed way on the meaning of the eucharistic bread — as he now proceeds to do.

Although the Corinthian Christians are many, by partaking of the Eucharistic loaf, they become one body. This unity, however, is not constituted 'horizontally', by the relations of Christians to each other. Rather, it comes about 'vertically', for the Eucharist offers *koinônia*, literally 'commonness', a common share, common participation, in the body of Christ. The relationship thus achieved is not simply a moral one, as if Christians were united only by faith in, and love of, the same object, namely Christ. More than this, it is 'ontological' relationship, where they share in the very reality of Christ's own life through feeding on him as a sacrificial victim. Paul does not hesitate to compare the Eucharistic *koinônia* to the union with the gods claimed in the pagan 'mystery-religions' of the period — the difference being that Paul held these gods to be demons, evil angels who lead people astray, whereas he identifies Jesus Christ as truly 'the Lord', *Kurios*, one with the true God who had revealed his Name, his personal reality, to Israel.

Having established his basic notion of the eucharistic *koinônia* as a communion with Christ which brings about fellowship between the Church's members, Paul goes on to rebuke the Corinthians for abuses in their celebrations of the Eucharist, which some of them trivialised as though it were an ordinary meal. In so adjuring them, Paul reminds his readers that the tradition about the Eucharist which he passed on to them he had himself received *apo tou Kuriou*, 'from (no less a person than) the Lord'.[35] There follows a somewhat different account of the institution narrative from the Marcan-Matthaean one — somewhat different, yet matching in all essentials. Some theologians, among whom we must count St Thomas, considered that when Paul spoke of the institution narrative as 'received from the Lord', he was claiming a special revelation of the events of the Last Supper, comparable to his Damascus Road experience. But most Catholic exegetes today regard the expression 'from the Lord' as the result of Paul's high doctrine of tradition. The tradition he had received from the apostolic community was 'holy tradition', stemming from the single Lord Jesus Christ who is both the earthly Jesus of the historic ministry and the exalted Christ of the Resurrection, sending the Holy Spirit: the one Lord of the Church. A handful of commentators with a background in patristic and Scholastic theology suggest, however, that whereas the basic facts about the Last Supper would have reached Paul by word of mouth from the tradition, their deeper significance may have come over to him mystically — that is, through supernaturally enabled contemplation. This would account for Paul's deepened understanding of the Eucharist as the foundation of the Church's unity: through receiving the Eucharistic body of Christ, we ourselves become his ecclesial body, the Church.

In his account of the institution of the Eucharist, Paul adds three nuances. First, his Jesus commands that the Eucharist be celebrated 'in his memory', *anamnêsis*, a phrase akin to rabbinic liturgical blessings which speak of the feasts God has given his people 'for joy and for a memorial'.[36] The concept of memorial here is not that of the present commemoration of a past event, which establishes a purely mental connection between the two. Instead, the past event becomes present in the here and now through the act of calling to mind. A fitting paraphrase of 'Do this as a memorial of me' would be, therefore, 'Do this to bring me into your present'. We commemorate Jesus eucharistically by inviting him to be present.

The second Pauline nuance lies in Jesus' insistence that this re-presentation of his sacrifice — this bringing into the present of a past reality — will be re-enacted continually over time. The phrase 'whenever', *hosakis*,[37] you drink it (the cup) implies a series of ritual events, many yet one, extending through history — as the Church of the first century would everywhere appreciate in establishing its eucharistic practice.

31

Finally, Paul adds his own comment that he who eats and drinks unworthily, *anaxios*, will be guilty, *enochos*, of the Lord's body and blood: he will have committed *lèse-majesté*, for the Greek supplies a technical term for assault on the person of the sovereign, the Roman law *reus majestatis*.[38]

In conclusion, we must cast a glance in the direction of Luke. Of all the evangelists, Luke most underlines the Passover nature of the Last Supper, which the Lucan Jesus actually refers to as 'this Passover'. But equally, Luke stresses the difference between Jewish Passover and Christian Eucharist: this he does by having Jesus give thanks at two quite distinct moments, first over the Passover food and drink, and then over the eucharistic gifts. His wording approximates to that of Paul, and just as the Pauline Jesus evidently expects the frequent liturgical celebration of the Eucharist, so the Lucan Church rises to meet this expectation. In the Acts of the Apostles, the other wing of Luke's diptych of a work, we find the Jerusalem Church zealous, in chapter 2, for the 'breaking of bread and the prayers', probably a technical phrase for the Eucharist.[39] Verse 46 may imply a daily celebration, while the seventeenth-century Flemish exegete Cornelius a Lapide took the phrase 'breaking of bread' to mean that communion was already, as a rule, under one kind, a claim supported by Jeremias who explains it in terms of the poverty of the primitive communities.

Drawing our investigation of the Eucharist in the New Testament to a close, it seems reasonable to ask, does the New Testament give to the Eucharist that enormous importance it has enjoyed in the later Church, especially in the Catholic tradition, where, as a slogan once graphically expressed things 'It is the Mass that matters'? The Eucharist does not perhaps loom so large in the pages of the New Testament as we might expect. The explanation may be provided by another hypothesis about the omission of the institution narrative in John, namely, the *disciplina arcani*, 'the discipline of the secret'. In both pagan and Jewish religion in Jesus' period, people drew a distinction between exoteric and esoteric teaching. Teaching for the public, for anyone who might happen to hear the speaker or to pick up scroll or papyrus, was not fully co-extensive with teaching for the initiated, the 'committed', those who had reached some kind of maturity and might be relied on to understand difficult truths and treat an intimate revelation of the divine with due reverence. Jesus himself acted on this distinction. The Synoptic gospels suggest that his esoteric teaching comprised his Messiahship, his prediction of the Passion and his prophecy of the end of the world and its signs. In the Gospel of John, a deeper meaning to Jesus' mission is disclosed in chapters 13 to 17, in the 'Farewell Discourse' spoken privately to his disciples.

The New Testament, and other early Christian writing, shows a related concern to safeguard the sacredness of the Eucharist from profanation. While, as we have seen, the Book of Acts uses pseudonyms for the Eucharist — breaking of bread, prayers, the Letter to the Hebrews reserves teaching about it to the mature. Again, the shorter (or 'Eastern') text of the Gospel of Luke reduces the institution narrative to a summary so cryptic as to be barely intelligible. If Loisy is correct, St John offers us his allegory of that event and story in the foot-washing. The principle involved was clearly stated by Hippolytus of Rome, writing shortly after the year 200. A self-consciously conservative author anxious not to go beyond what he terms 'the apostolic tradition', Hippolytus ends his section on Baptism and Eucharist by saying:

One shall not describe this to any but the faithful.[40]

John Henry Newman, to whom this sense of reserve was precious, would later point out, on the foundation of his own patristic researches, the manner of this discipline: not a rule, canon or law, a systematic norm, but a 'feeling and a principle'.[41] It is to the Fathers' understanding of the Eucharist that we must now turn.

2

The Eucharist in the Age of the Fathers

In dealing with the patristic theology of the Eucharist, I propose to divide the material which has come down to us into three blocks: the words of the Fathers about the real presence, about the real sacrifice and about the relationship between the Eucharist and the Church.

The Eucharist as presence

First of all, the real presence. In the period before the First Council of Nicaea, assembled in 325, we encounter three kinds of language for what is given to us in the Eucharist. In the first place, we can overhear the Fathers using a relatively vague language, which speaks in rather general terms of a spiritual gift. Thus the Alexandrian writer Origen (c.185-254) refers to the 'flesh and blood of the Word' as 'drink and refreshment' given by God to 'the whole human race'.[1] The (third century?) *Egyptian Church Order* describes the purpose of the eucharistic consecration as

> the holiness (of the communicants), and for filling them with the Holy Spirit, and for strengthening faith in truth, that they may glorify and praise you.[2]

In the second place, we come across statements to the effect that the eucharistic bread and wine are the *sumbolon*, 'symbol', or *figura*, 'figure', of Christ's body and blood. Thus Clement of Alexandria (c.150-215) remarks that 'Scripture called wine the mystic *sumbolon* of the sacred blood',[3] while the North African Tertullian (c.160-225) explains the words 'This is my body' as 'This is the *figura* of my body'.[4] How can such language be reconciled, if at all, with the exegesis of the Institution Narrative offered in the last chapter, where

34

it was maintained that, at the Last Supper, Jesus *identified* his body and blood with the Passover bread and wine, rather than declaring them to be mere tokens of his sacrificial death? The word *sumbolon* in ancient times had very different connotations from those it bears today. The (Lutheran) historian of doctrine Adolf von Harnack (1851-1930) put the matter clearly. In his history of dogma he writes:

> What we nowadays understand by 'symbol' is a thing which is not that which it represents; at that time, 'symbol' denoted a thing which in some kind of way really is what it signifies. What we now call 'symbol' is something wholly different from what was so called by the ancient Church.[5]

Evidence for the truth of this statement will be forthcoming if we look briefly at how the Latin Church in Tertullian's time used his favourite phrase for the eucharistic gifts: *figura*. Where Paul says of his Lord, in the Letter to the Philippians, that he was 'in the form, *morphê*, of God',[6] the old Latin Bible, picking up the quasi-aesthetic connotations of that word, has it that the Son was in God's *figura*.[7] Again, the Latin version of the Creed used in Gaul translates *sarkôthenta*, 'and was made flesh', with the words, 'and took the *figura* of man'.[8] Tertullian himself, when stressing that the Word truly took flesh in Mary's womb, speaks of him as taking *caro figuratus*: not 'figurative flesh', evidently, but the distinctively formed flesh of a human being. So, just as *sumbolon* means the manifestation of a reality in a fresh medium, *figura* signifies the distinctiveness of a reality. And similarly, when Tertullian calls the Eucharist a representation of Christ's body and blood, we must bear in mind that, in general, *repraesentare* means to make present (re-present) that which is now unseen.[9]

But the symbolist language used for the eucharistic presence in ante-Nicene authors might be capable of another, more reductionist, interpretation were it not for the fact that in the same period people are also using frankly realist language at the same time. Ignatius of Antioch criticises his Docetist opponents who

> held aloof from the Eucharist and prayer because they do not believe that the Eucharist is the flesh of our Saviour, Jesus Christ.[10]

Justin Martyr (c.100–c.165) in his *Apologia* explains for the benefit of pagan readers:

> This food is called among us the Eucharist, and of it no one is allowed to partake unless he believes that our teaching is true and has been bathed in the waters for the forgiveness of sins and for regeneration, and is living as Christ commanded. For we do not receive it as common bread or common drink, but, just as Jesus Christ our Saviour, made flesh by the Word of God, has both flesh and blood for our salvation, so also we have been taught that the food over which thanksgiving has been made, by the prayer of the Word that is from him, that food — from which our blood and flesh are by assimilation nourished — is both the flesh and the blood of the Jesus who was made flesh.[11]

Again, Irenaeus of Lyons (c.130–c.200) takes for granted the reality of Christ's presence in the consecrated elements, the better to argue against the Gnostics that the bodily humanity assumed by the Word at the Incarnation was real, just as will be, one day, our own bodily resurrection.

> As the bread of the earth, receiving the invocation of God, is no longer common bread but the Eucharist, made up of two things, an earthly and a heavenly, so also our bodies, partaking of the Eucharist, are no longer corruptible, having the hope of the resurrection to eternity.[12]

More evidence for patristic attachment to a real presence comes from an almost exactly contemporary inscription also found, like Irenaeus' pastorate, in Roman Gaul, at Autun

36

in Burgundy. Speaking of Christ under the well-known acronym of the fish — taken from the initial letters of the Greek words for 'Jesus Christ, Son of God, Saviour (*Ichthus: Iêsous Christos Theou Huios Sôtêr*), the Autun inscription refers to him as placed in communicants' hands:

> Nourish, beloved, your soul with the ever-flowing waters of everlasting Wisdom. Receive the honey-sweet Food of the Saviour of the holy; Eat, drink, having the Fish in your hands.[13]

Or again, Tertullian speaks of the consecrated Eucharist as *sanctum*, 'that holy thing'.[14] He advises great care that no drop of the wine or fragment of the bread should fall to the ground.[15] It is, he says, the Lord's own body which the communicant receives in church or reserves for his communion at home,[16] and even in unworthy communions it is this body of the Lord which wicked hands approach and wicked men outrage and offend.[17]

Still in North Africa, but a generation later, Cyprian of Carthage, exhorting the faithful to stand firm under persecution, says:

> Let us arm our right hand with the sword of the Spirit, so that it may bravely reject the deadly sacrifices of the pagans, and that the hand which, mindful of the Eucharist, receives the body of the Lord, may embrace the Lord himself, obtaining in the life to come the reward of his heavenly crowns.[18]

Moving on to the post-Nicene period, the age of the great Councils, we find an increasing predominance of realist language over either the indefinite or the symbolist accounts of the Gifts, as well as the beginnings of a theological attempt to explore the relationship between the material elements and Jesus Christ in his divine-human reality. As to the first of these developments, we find Athanasius of Alexandria (c.296–c.373), in his *Commentary on Matthew*, stimulated by the saying of Jesus (to the Syro-Phoenician woman) on not giving what is holy to the dogs. Addressing rhetorically the Church's deacons, the great confessor admonishes them:

> You also, deacon, take care that you do not give to the unworthy the purple of the sinless body.[19]

And Pope Saint Leo the Great (d. 461), in a sermon, advises his people:

> You ought so to partake at the Holy Table as to have no doubt at all concerning the reality of the body and blood of Christ. For what is taken in the mouth is that which is believed by faith, and it is vain for them to respond 'Amen' [to the formula of distribution or administration] who dispute against that which is taken.[20]

We know from Cyril of Jerusalem's (c.315-386) *Catechetical Lectures* that explicit teaching on the real presence formed part of the normal instructions given to converts awaiting their initiation into the mysteries.

> The bread and wine of the Eucharist [says St Cyril] were simple bread and wine before the invocation of the holy and adorable Trinity, but when the invocation has taken place the bread becomes the body of Christ and the wine the blood of Christ. . .[21]

> The seeming bread is not bread even though it is sensible to the taste, but the body of Christ, and the seeming wine is not wine, even though the taste will have it so, but the blood of Christ.[22]

The practica of the patristic Church is also important in this connection. Cyril's instructions on how one should actually receive holy communion are often cited:

> Make your left hand a throne for your right, as for that which is to receive a king. And, hollowing your palm, receive the body of Christ, saying over it the 'Amen'. With due attention, sanctify your eyes by the

sight of the holy body, and partake of it, taking care not to lose any part of it; for whatever you would lose would evidently be a loss to you from one of your own members.

And Cyril continues, by asking:

Tell me, if any one gave you grains of gold, would you not hold them with all care taking heed lest you should lose any of them and suffer loss? Will you not much more carefully be on your guard lest a crumb fall from you of what is more valuable than gold and precious stones?

And, *à propos* of the chalice, he has this to say:

After you have made your communion in the body of Christ, draw near also to the cup of his blood, not stretching out your hands but bowing, and in an attitude of reverence and worship saying the 'Amen', hallow yourself by partaking also of the blood of Christ.[23]

At the end of the fifth century special devotion comes to be paid to the blessed Sacrament — that is, to Christ in the sacrament — within the Church's liturgy, a liturgy which, in itself, is not, of course, directed to Christ but to the Father, through the Son, in the Holy Spirit. The *Agnus Dei* of the Roman rite is such a devotional prayer addressed to Christ really present in the Eucharist. As the Anglican liturgical historian Gregory Dix pointed out, the crucial moment in the development of eucharistic piety comes not with the emergence of extra-liturgical devotions in the later Middle Ages but with the flowering of intra-liturgical devotion in the patristic period itself.[24] Archaeological evidence suggests that the practice of reserving the Blessed Sacrament, and even of keeping a lamp lighted before it begins at that time, as does the custom whereby bishops and missionary monks carried the sacrament in some kind of receptacle, usually a pyx around the neck.[25] In the early twentieth century, such theologians as Anscar Vonier and Maurice de la Taille will stress that eucharistic devotion is the extension of that moment of the eucharistic celebration which lies between the consecration and the communion.[26] We owe this feature of developed Catholic practice to the sense, then, of the real presence manifested by the patristic Church.

Yet, despite the settled convictions of East and West on this score, symbolist terminology for the presence continued. We have already observed the operation of the terms *sumbolon* and *figura* but new ones were entering into use at their side. In the West, the term *signum*, 'sign', became popular, and in the East *eikôn*, 'image', and *antitupos*, 'antitype'. Thus Augustine (354-430), in one of his anti-Manichaean writings, remarks

> The Lord did not hesitate to say, 'This is my body' when he gave the sign of his body.[27]

Another writer against the Manichees, Adamantios (*fl.* c.330), asks in the course of his defence of the reality of Jesus' body:

> If, as these men say, he was fleshless and bloodless, of what flesh or of what blood was it that he gave the images, in the bread and the cup, when he commanded these disciples to commemorate him by means of these?[28]

Such *façons de parler* troubled other theologians. Macarius of Magnesia, writing around 400, mentions those who spoke of the Eucharist in a way he himself repudiated:

> It is not a type of the body and type of the blood, as some whose minds are blinded have foolishly said, but really the body and blood of Christ.[29]

If, as Harnack suggested, the ancient idea of a symbol was that of the manifestation of a reality in a fresh medium, that idea was patent, clearly, of development in either of two directions. Either one could stress the continuity and self-identity of the reality concerned in its own being and in its manifestation in the new medium, or, alternatively, one might emphasise the novelty of the medium, and so come to lay the greater weight on difference and discontinuity.[30]

In the East, the use of such terms as *eikôn, tupos* and *antitupos* for the consecrated elements was cut short during the Iconoclast controversy of the eighth and ninth centuries. The opponents of the images argued, among other things, that the Church has no need of paintings of Jesus Christ since she already possesses his image in the Eucharist. The acts of the Iconoclast synod held in Constantinople in 754 declare:

> When he was about to give himself up of his own free choice to his glorious and life-giving death, he took the bread and blessed it, and gave thanks and broke it, and gave it to them, saying, 'Take, eat, for the remission of sins; this is my body'. In like manner also he gave them the cup and said, 'This is my blood: do this for my memorial'. Thus no other form under heaven was chosen by him, and no other figure can be an image of his incarnation.[31]

But the seventh ecumenical council, Nicaea II, meeting in 787 to restore the icons, rejected this argument in no uncertain terms. The Iconophile bishops heard gladly a speech by a deacon, Epiphanius, who declared of the Iconoclast leaders:

> These fine fellows, in their desire to do away with regard for the venerable images, have brought in another image, which is not an image but body and blood.[32]

And the speaker maintained, with some exaggeration:

> Never did the Lord or the apostles or the Fathers call the bloodless sacrifice which is offered by the priest an image but the body itself and the blood itself.[33]

What the seventh ecumenical Council did consider

41

legitimate, however, was calling the elements 'antitypes' —
in effect, images — *prior* to their consecration, a usage which
St John Damascene (c.675-c.749) had allowed some years
previously.[34]

This Eastern controversy had the effect of promoting
veneration of the bread and wine before the consecration
as images of Christ, something which can still be witnessed
at the Byzantine liturgy today. When the prepared, but still
unconsecrated, elements are brought to the sanctuary at the
'Great Entrance', the people bow, sign themselves and
sometimes make a prostration, the self-same ritual gestures
employed before the icons.[35] The Western Church, on the
other hand, was comparatively untouched by the Iconoclast
crisis, so that Augustine's description of the Eucharist as
a sign was not called into question this side of Ravenna.

How did the patristic Church understand the relation
between the physical elements and the real presence of Jesus
Christ? Many writers spoke in very general terms of the
heightened significance or efficacy of the elements after
consecration — comparing this to what happens to water
in baptism, the chrism at its blessing for sacramental use,
to a man in ordination, or even to an altar at its liturgical
installation: thus, for instance, the fourth century Gregory
of Nyssa's (c.330-c.395) sermon 'On the Baptism of Christ'.[36]
The natural sense of such a comparison would be that the
consecrated elements are simply an instrument divinely used
for the realising of some spiritual purpose. Placed side by
side with other passages, even in the same authors, the texts
speak somewhat differently. Comparison of the gifts with
other sacraments or sacramentals was not intended, it seems,
to be an exhaustive account of the eucharistic truth. For
the eucharistic elements must be more than an instrument
if they are identified with that which they are the means
of bestowing.

Following the Anglican historian of eucharistic doctrine,
Darwell Stone, the Fathers, in throwing light on the relation
of the presence to the elements, fall naturally into two groups.

There are those who stress the abiding reality of the bread and wine; and those who affirm a change in the elements themselves. Broadly, and in terms not only of geography but of the christological schools of thought which developed in the emerging patriarchal churches, the first group are Antiochenes, and at an extreme, Nestorians. The second group are Alexandrians, and at an extreme, Monophysites.[37] (As so often, the Roman popes were somewhere in the middle.)

Typical of the Antiochenes is the notion that the bread of the Eucharist remains bread after consecration, just as the embodied humanity taken by the Word remains a human body throughout his incarnate life and is so still, after the Ascension. Thus in the fifth century dialogue *Eranistes*, 'The Beggarman', by Theodoret of Cyr (c.393–c.446), the extreme Cyrillian (Eutychian) heretic agrees with the 'Catholic' (the Antiochene) that after the consecration the elements are Christ's body and blood, but he also disagrees with him in a vital respect. The Eutychian maintains that, after the Ascension, Christ's body is changed into the divine nature so as to be no longer a human body and that, similarly, after the consecration, the elements are changed into the body and blood of Christ in such a way that no longer are they bread and wine. The 'Catholic' maintains that, after the Ascension, Christ's body remains a human body, though now incorruptible and glorious, and that, similarly, after the consecration, the eucharistic elements continue to be bread and wine in 'substance, figure and form', though they are also the body and blood of Christ.[38] Much the same argumentation is found in Pope Gelasius' (d.496) treatise *On the Two Natures in Christ,* written to defend the Chalcedonian settlement in Christology.[39] Removed from its context of gradually developing doctrine, this sounds like the (Lutheran) theological doctrine of the presence known as 'consubstantiation'.

On the other hand, other Fathers tend to minimise any continuance of the elements of bread and wine after the consecration, and to approximate to some form of the doctrine later known as 'transubstantiation'. In the *Catechetical Lectures,* Cyril of Jerusalem declares:

> Once at Cana in Galilee he changed water into wine by his own will; is it incredible that he should change, *metaballein,* wine into blood?[40]

More definitely, Gregory of Nyssa proposes that, by the consecration, the elements are 'trans-made', *metapoieisthai,* and 'trans-elemented', *metastoicheiousthai,* into the body and blood of the Lord. Just as, in ordinary biological life, bread and wine are progressively taken up and transformed into our flesh and blood through being consumed, digested and assimilated, so it is, Gregory explains, with the eucharistic elements. They become Christ's body and blood, but in a single moment of time.[41] Their constituent elements, *stoicheia,* are re-arranged under a new form, *eidos.* John Chrysostom (c.347–407) speaks in a similar way of the divine Word re-ordering, *metarrythmizein,*[42] the gifts and transforming, *metaskeuazein,* them.[43]

Here in Chrysostom the *agent* of the eucharistic transformation is God the Word. Actually, however, Chrysostom, like many of the Fathers, speaks somewhat ambivalently about the source of the eucharistic transformation: is it the Son, or the Spirit? (Clearly, the *ultimate* source, as with all divine action, must be the Father.) Symptomatically, he refers the consecration of the elements sometimes to the *epiklêsis,* the prayer for the descent of the Spirit, sometimes to the words of the institution narrative, stemming from the Son. This ambivalence is entirely characteristic of the patristic tradition in general, though there is a tendency for the Eastern fathers, whether Greek or Syriac, to treat the *epiklêsis* as in the fullest sense consecratory, and to mention the institution narrative only by way of complement, while the Western Fathers — whose liturgies did not, in any case, always include a sharply defined *epiklêsis,* or one concerned explicitly with the coming of the

Spirit — privilege the institution narrative, the words of the great High Priest, and treat the *epiklêsis* as, by and large, 'post-consecratory' in significance. For the Fathers at large, or so it seems, the anaphora (the eucharistic prayer) was consecratory in its entirety, though with its sanctifying force concentrated at two high points. Accordingly, for them, both Son and Spirit are involved, with and from the Father, the Fount of the Godhead, in the eucharistic transformation.[44]

Finally, on the real presence, we should note the valiant effort of the Fathers to set their eucharistic doctrine in a wider soteriological context. Clearly, the real presence is not theologically intelligible as a bare metaphysical fact. It must be given us for some end, some purpose. Gregory of Nyssa's *Catechetical Oration* illustrates the concern of the Fathers for the rationale of the eucharistic presence, as of the sacraments in general. In the latter, for Gregory, what was once accomplished for humankind in general by the Incarnation is now accomplished continuously and for individual persons. Since the human being is composed of body and soul those who wish to place themselves in the way of salvation must lay hold of Christ by both soul and body. Because human nature has been poisoned through the body, the gate by which all experience reaches us, the antidote to the poison must also be received in a bodily way. This antidote is that one only body which conquered death and now flourishes as the first-fruits of new life.[45]

But of course the eucharistic event should not be thought of as parallel to the saving Incarnation (and its climax in the Death and Resurrection) in the sense of an independent channel of access to the graciousness of God. On the contrary, the eucharistic gifts are radically dependent upon those mysteries of Christ for their effect. This explains why, in the succeeding fifth century, Cyril of Alexandria (d.444) connected his teaching on the Eucharist with the main theme of his life — the single hypostasis of the Word Incarnate, and the deeds done in and by that personhood for our salvation. As St Cyril insists, the value of the Eucharist derives from, and depends on, the hypostatic or personal union which bonds together the divine and human natures of the Word. The flesh received by communicants in the Eucharist has its life-giving properties not because it is the flesh of a human being, however holy, but because it is the flesh assumed by the person of the Word.[46] Church historians have suggested that popular support of Cyril's theology, over against that of Nestorius, was forthcoming mainly because Cyril could show that the eucharistic gifts were life-giving, and Nestorius could not.[47]

The Eucharist as sacrifice
Let us turn now to the patristic fate of the theme of eucharistic sacrifice. The ante-Nicene age was marked by a repudiation of what contemporaries called 'carnal sacrifices'. In some cases, early Christian writers held that, by offering such sacrifices, the Jews of the Old Testament had quite misunderstood the commands or wishes of God: this was the view of the pseudonymous Epistle of Barnabas.[48] Somewhat more reasonably, Justin and Tertullian saw animal sacrifice as genuinely willed by God for the people of the ancient Covenant, but only as a concession to Jewish 'hardness of heart'; they concluded that it belonged to a dispensation now superseded in Christ.[49] The general consensus of the early patristic period (which owes much, of course, to criticism of popular attitudes to the Israelite cultus by some of the prophets, as well as to the 'fulfilment theology' of the Letter to the Hebrews) is well summed up in the apologist Athenagoras who wrote:

> He who is Maker and Father of this universe needs not blood nor fact nor the sweet smell of flowers and incense, since he himself is the perfect Odour who needs nothing from within nor from without... What are whole burnt-offerings to me, since God needs them not?[50]

But what, then, had taken the place of the sacrifices of

the Jewish past? The most obvious answer is, the totality of Christian faith, life and worship. This is what we find in Clement of Alexandria's portrait of the Christian:

> All his life is a holy festival. His sacrifices consist of prayers and praises and the reading of the Scriptures before dining, and psalms and hymns during dinner and before going to bed, and also of prayers again during the night. By these things he unites himself with the heavenly choir, being enlisted in it for ever-mindful contemplation. . .

And Clement adds that the perfect Christian is also

> acquainted with that other sacrifice which consists in the free gift both of instruction and of money among those who are in need.[51]

But since the entire pattern of Christian life and worship, with its constituent elements of prayer, mission and almsgiving, could thus be spoken of in sacrificial terms, so too might the Eucharist. Insofar as the Eucharist was the central act of the Church's life, it was also her central sacrifice — in this generalised and diffuse sense of that word. Justin and the author of the *Didache* refer to the Eucharist as *thusia*, a sacrifice, or even as '*the* sacrifice' of Christians, while Irenaeus calls it 'the pure sacrifice', the 'new oblation of the new Covenant'. He was consciously concerned to defend the use of sacrificial language for the Eucharist against (apparently) critics:

> Oblation as such, *genus oblationum*, is not condemned, for there are oblations among us, as well as among the Jews, sacrifices in the Church as well as among the ancient people of God; it is only the way, *species*, of sacrifice which is changed, since the offering is now made not by slaves but by free men.[52]

The notion that, if the whole of the Christian life is a sacrifice in God's honour, then the Eucharist, as the centre of that life, must be the sacrifice *par excellence,* was encouraged by early Christian interpretation of Malachi 1:11:

> From the rising of the sun to its setting my name is great among the nations, and in every place incense is offered to my name, and a pure offering; for my name is great among the nations, says the Lord of hosts.

Patristic writers commonly saw in this text a prophecy of the Eucharist.[53]

But did the ante-Nicene fathers regard the Eucharist as a sacrifice in any sense specific to itself? Was it simply a matter of the Eucharist focusing the sacrificial quality of Christian existence at large, or was there something more? The texts open two perspectives on how the Eucharist may be sacrificially distinctive. In the first place, they link the Eucharist in a special way with the sacrifice of the Cross. Justin remarks of the eucharistic bread that our Lord commanded us to offer it for an *anamnêsis* of the Passion.[54] Cyprian makes explicit what may be involved when he writes:

> If our Lord and God Christ Jesus is himself the high priest of God the Father, and offered himself as a sacrifice to the Father, commanding this to be done for a memorial of himself — then certainly the *sacerdos* [literally, the priest, but more probably the bishop here] truly performs his office in the place of Christ, imitating that which Christ did, and offering in the Church to God the Father a real and complete sacrifice.[55]

But if these texts link the Eucharist with Christ's Passion, others associate the eucharistic sacrifice with the intercession of the risen and glorified Christ. Irenaeus, in close connection with his assertion of the sacrificial character of the Eucharist, explains that there is an altar, temple and tabernacle 'in the heavens', whither our prayers and offerings are directed: a heavenly sacrifice, then, in which the earthly, sacramental act of the Eucharist participates.[56] This heavenly sacrifice is Christ's permanent offering of the sacred humanity which he took at the Incarnation and sacrificed in his dying. To it the Church joins herself by means of the Eucharist. Origen describes Christ as presenting in the heavenly sanctuary all the sacrificial oblations which Christians on earth bring to God's altar. Christians 'come to Christ, the true high priest' who reconciled us to the Father, and hear him saying, 'This is my blood'.[57]

In the post-Nicene age, sacrificial language for the Eucharist becomes more insistent. At the same time, in Augustine, a reflective theology of the Eucharist as sacrifice makes its first bow. First of all, then, sacrificial language is used more frequently and with greater emphasis. The Euchologion (missal) of Serapion prays at the Liturgy:

> O Lord of Hosts, fill this sacrifice with your power and participation; for to you have we offered this living sacrifice, this bloodless offering.[58]

Cyril of Jerusalem calls the Eucharist 'that sacrifice of propitiation', 'the holy and most awful sacrifice'.[59] In the West, Ambrose counts it among the duties of the ordained 'to offer sacrifice for the people', and declares that Christ 'is himself offered on earth when the body of Christ is offered'.[60] Augustine calls the Eucharist at different times 'the sacrifice of our redemption', 'the sacrifice of the Mediator', 'the sacrifice of peace', 'the sacrifice of the body and blood of the Lord', 'the sacrifice of the Church'.[61]

As earlier, the Eucharist is seen as a sharing in both the sacrifice of Calvary and in Jesus' post-Resurrection offering of his humanity to the Father. John Chrysostom exhorts his people to attend the Liturgy with reverence and devotion since

> He who was nailed to the Cross, we are to see slaughtered and sacrificed as a Lamb... He was slain for you, and you neglect to see him sacrificed... Think what that is which has been shed. It is blood, blood

which blotted out the handwriting of our sins, blood which cleansed your soul, which washed away the stain, which triumphed over the principalities and powers... Reverence, then, this Table, of which we all have communion, Christ slain on our behalf, the sacrifice that is laid upon it.[62]

In other words, our communion is with Christ as sacrificial Victim, sacramentally present upon the alter. But since the Eucharist is a sacramental sacrifice, pertaining to the order of signs, it should be possible to say by what aspect of the liturgical action the sacrifice is signified. Gregory Nazianzen seems to anticipate Thomas Aquinas' idea that the crucial ritual moment is the separate consecration of the bread and wine, for the Cappadocian doctor speaks of the 'bloodless cutting' whereby the Lord's body and blood are 'severed' by the 'sword' of the priest's voice.[63] However, it would be wrong to imagine that the sacramental sacrifice thus reduces the heavenly sacrifice to the dimensions of our worship. Rather does it extend, or raise up, our worship to become a participation in the heavenly sacrifice: the motif of union with the exalted High Priest already announced in the ante-Nicene period. Let us hear John Chrysostom again:

We have our victim in heaven, our priest in heaven, our sacrifice in heaven... When you see the Lord sacrificed and lying as an oblation, and the priest standing by the sacrifice and praying, and all things reddened with that precious blood, do you think that you are still among men and standing on earth?[64]

But, apart from the continuation and intensification of themes from the age before Nicaea, the later Fathers also show the beginnings of an explicit theology of sacrifice, and here is where we turn to Augustine. First of all, Augustine offers us a reflective general concept of sacrifice. In Book X of *The City of God*, the North African doctor enquires whether

50

there is a kind of worship which can be offered to God alone, as distinct from worship that might be offered, legitimately, to angels, or even to human beings. He thinks there is, and, taking up a word from the Greek Bible, the Septuagint, he calls it *latreia*. The whole Christian life should manifest such *latreia*, and Augustine expresses this *desideratum* in sacrificial language.

> We offer to him on the altar of the heart the sacrifice of humility and praise.[65]

He justifies calling purely internal acts — movements of the heart and mind — 'sacrifices' by defining sacrifice as

> every act by which it comes about that we cleave to God in holy fellowship — directed, that is, to the First Good by which we are truly made happy.[66]

However, this does not entail that the only true sacrifices are such sheerly interior actions. As Augustine points out, we can offer God *latreia* either in ourselves or in a public act of worship, for the excellent reason that we are both individually God's temples (since we have the Holy Spirit indwelling us through grace) and corporately the temple which is the body of his Son. Normally, normatively, indeed, a sacrifice will be part and parcel of the public world of shared symbolic activity to which we belong through ritual. Augustine wants to preserve, however, the all-important connection with an interior cleaving to God as our final end, so he describes the public sacrificial act as *visibile invisibilis sacrificii sacramentum*, 'the visible sacrament of an invisible sacrifice'.[67]

And this Augustine now identifies with that:

> sacrifice which the Church continually celebrates in the sacrament of the altar, ... where it is shown to the Church that she herself is offered in the offering which she presents to God.[68]

In the offering of praise in the bread and wine placed on

the liturgical altar, the Church understands herself not only as making an offering to God but, more deeply, as being an offering — a spiritual sacrifice, a corporate human existence made over to God, ordered and directed to him. But if, we may ask, in the eucharistic sacrifice it is the *Church* which is offered to God, what has happened to the Saviour Jesus Christ and his *self*-offering on the Cross? How does this liturgical sacrifice, which the Church both offers and is, relate to Christ?

Augustine considers this in two steps. Both concern Christ as mediator between God and us, but one touches the divine aspect of his mediatory activity, the other the human. In the *form of God:* Christ receives the Church's sacrifice and integrates it with his own self-offering to the Father, a self-offering which is at once his own very existence as the Logos, the Word, the Son, and the act accomplished on the Cross, the historical expression of Christ's being as 'God from God' in space and time.

> The whole of the redeemed city, that is to say, the congregation and fellowship of the saints, is offered to God as a universal sacrifice through the great priest who offered himself in his suffering for us — so that we might be the body of so great a Head.

But then, secondly, in the *form of a servant:* Christ does not receive the Church's sacrifice; he *is* it. On the Cross, he was not only the offerer of a sacrifice; he was also what was offered. As Augustine explains, though Christ, 'the true mediator', receives the sacrifice in the form of God in union with the Father, with whom he is one God, yet as man, in the form of a servant, he

> preferred to be himself the sacrifice, rather than to receive it.[69]

Thus he became on the Cross both priest and oblation, the one who offers and the offering.

With these preliminaries of a christological doctrine of

52

salvation established, Augustine is able to explain how the primary sacrifice of Calvary is related to the secondary sacrifice of the Church. In the first place, the Church's sacrifice is the sacramental symbolisation of the sacrifice of Christ. Christ founded the Eucharist as a sacramental sign of his own sacrifice, so that the Church, in offering bread and wine, offers not only herself but Christ as well. And in the second place, by celebrating this sacramental symbol, the Church learns how to insert her self-offering into that of the only Mediator. In a masterly fashion, Augustine brings together the idea that the Church offers herself in the Eucharist with the notion that she offers Christ there by proposing that, in the eucharistic liturgy, the Church learns how to integrate her self-offering into Christ's, just as Christ's human self-offering was integrated into the divine self-offering of the Word. As the *De Civitate Dei* continues:

> He [Christ] intended the daily sacrifice of the Church to be the sacramental symbol of this [his own sacrifice]; for the Church, being the body of which he is the Head, learns to offer herself through him.[70]

And Augustine concludes, referring both to Calvary and the Eucharist at once:

> This is the true sacrifice; and the sacrifice of holy men in earlier times were many different symbols of it. This one sacrifice was prefigured by many rites, just as many words are used to refer to one thing, to emphasise a point without inducing boredom. This was the supreme sacrifice, and the true sacrifice, and all the false sacrifices yielded to it.[71]

Because the sacramental sacrifice incorporates the self-offering of the 'whole redeemed city' into Christ's self-offering, Augustine believes that it benefits both the living and the dead. On her death-bed, his mother had asked to be remembered at God's altar, and in Book X of the *Confessions* Augustine recalls how *sacrificium pretii nostri*, the 'sacrifice of our redemption', was offered for her at the grave-side before her body was placed in its tomb. And generalising this act of piety to the many, he remarks in the *Enchiridion*, or 'Handbook of Christian Doctrine', that the Mediator's sacrifice is offered for the souls of the dead through the good offices of the living.

The Eucharist as foundation of the Church

So far as the patristic testimony is concerned, it remains to consider the third main motif which the New Testament origins put forth: after the real presence and the real sacrifice comes the Eucharist's consequent relation to the Church. Various Fathers comment at some length on Paul's statement in 1 Corinthians that

> we who are many are all one body since we all partake of the one bread.[72]

Here the homilies of John Chrysostom and Theodoret are, it may be, outstanding. But the idea that the Church's unity takes its foundation from the Eucharist is, above all, Augustine's. For Augustine, the *virtus*, the special 'virtue' or 'power' of the Eucharist is unity. After all, the eucharistic presence has the aim of uniting believers to each other through their union with Christ; the eucharistic sacrifice unites the whole redeemed city to the Father by introducing our self-offering into that of the mediator. By feeding on the eucharistic body of Christ, we become, then, his ecclesial body — what would later be termed his 'mystical body', a phrase which, as Pope Pius XII would insist in the encyclical *Mystici Corporis*, is by no means simply a metaphor. Augustine's fullest account is found in Sermon 272:

> If you wish to understand the body of Christ, hear the apostle speaking to the faithful, 'You are the body and members of Christ'. If then you are Christ's body and members, it is your mystery which is laid upon the Lord's Table. You receive your own mystery. When

[to the formula of administration] you answer 'Amen', you answer to that which you are, and, in answering, you assent. For you hear the words, 'The body of Christ' and you answer 'Amen'. Be a member of the body of Christ that the Amen may be true... Remember that the bread is not made from one grain but from many. When you were exorcised [during the catechumenate] you were, so to speak, ground. When you were baptised, you were, so to speak, sprinkled. When you received the fire of the Holy Spirit [in Confirmation] you were, so to speak, baked. Be what you see, and receive what you are.

This, Augustine says, the apostle had in mind when speaking of the bread. Turning then to the chalice:

Though he does not say in so many words how we are to understand the cup, nevertheless, he shows with sufficient clearness. Brethren, recall whence the wine is made. Many grapes hang on the cluster, but the juice of the grapes is gathered together in unity.

And Augustine concludes this symbolic theology of eucharistic initiation into the common life of the Church:

So also the Lord Christ signified us, willed that we belong to him and consecrated on his Table the mystery of our peace and unity.[73]

But if the celebration of the Eucharist lies at the foundation of the Church, herself the 'sacrament of the Kingdom' (as the Second Vatican Council will put it, in recovering the insights of this eucharistic ecclesiology), then the eucharistic liturgy must surely be — as the preface to this book has intimated — the icon and foretaste of the feast of the Kingdom. In the Synoptic gospels, as we have noted, an eschatological dimension to the Eucharist is revealed in the comment of the Lord at the Supper that he will not drink again of the fruit of the vine until he drinks it anew in the Kingdom of his Father. The Church Fathers came to no true consensus about his meaning. For Irenaeus[74] and (especially) Augustine, that saying is fulfilled only in the future, beyond the time of the Church's sacramental existence. For Jerome of Bethlehem, in sharp contrast, its meaning was achieved in the Eucharist itself.[76] But a wide variety of authors, both Eastern and Western, trod a *via media*, which is that of the liturgies themselves.[77] They present the Eucharist as in the words of the English Methodist student of this theme, Geoffrey Wainright:

> an effective promise, to those who receive it rightly, of participation in the full and final reality of which it is a taste.[78]

For the sacramentaries of the Western rite in the patristic age, the Eucharist is the image of what will be made manifest; the celebration under appearances of what we shall receive in reality; the prefiguration of the full, unending enjoyment of our Lord's Godhead; the possession in hope of what we shall truly enjoy in heaven; a tasting of the joy that heaven will fulfil.[79] Nor do the Eastern liturgies speak in different tones:

> Even, or rather precisely, in those liturgies which are freest in calling the eucharistic meal already a heavenly reality, there is a strong awareness that future blessings still remain in store.[80]

The ultimate explanation for this lies in the Church's conviction about the real presence of Christ. In the Eucharist we are given an anticipation of the final coming of the Lord, in both judgment and blessing. Hence the importance, for liturgical life in the patristic age, of the celebration of Sunday, the 'weekly Easter', looking forward as this does to the Parousia and the general Resurrection; as also of celebrating the Eucharist in the eastward position, for he who is to return is, as Luke 1:78 declares in a Canticle used in the

Church's Morning Prayer, the 'Day-Star' [literally, the East, *Anatolê*], 'from on high'.

These implications of the Holy Eucharist were not lost on the mediaeval divines of Western Catholicism to whose eucharistic doctrine we must now turn.

3

The Mediaevals on the Nature of the Real Presence

In considering the development of eucharistic doctrine in the Latin Church between the age of the Fathers and the classical moment of St Thomas, we encounter two fundamental issues. First, what is the mode of Christ's presence in the Eucharist? Here we shall find maximalists and minimalists, or, if you will, literalists and symbolists, in debate sometimes enlightening, sometimes merely, alas, acrimonious, until, with the emergence of the concept of transubstantiation, a satisfactory resolution is achieved. Although transubstantiation enters the conciliar tradition with the Fourth Lateran Council in 1215, it flowers into theological light with the *tertia pars* of Thomas' *Summa Theologiae*, written in 1272. The second issue occupying the centre of the stage in the early mediaeval period concerns the purpose, aim or salvific rationale of the Eucharist. As the Cappadocians had already realised, the real presence cannot be left as a bare metaphysical fact. It must possess its own 'finality', its own intrinsic purpose within the economy of salvation. As we shall see in the next chapter, two views of what this purpose might be existed side by side. One concentrated on the mystical aspect of the Eucharist, and saw its purpose as the achieving of spiritual union between Christ and the believer. The other emphasised the ecclesial dimension, locating the finality of the presence in the unification of the whole Church by charity. These two perspectives are conveniently brought together in Thomas' assertion that the ultimate reference of the Eucharist is the mystical unity of the Church of Christ — thus showing that the 'vertical' and 'horizontal' perspectives are not rivals or competitors but complement each other.

Paschasius and Ratramnus

But our task in this chapter is to investigate the developing discussion in the early mediaeval Church on the *nature* of the real presence. The debate's starting-point may be dated to around 830 when a monk-theologian of the Benedictine abbey of Corbie in eastern France, Paschasius Radbert (c.790-865), was asked to produce a comprehensive exposition of the Eucharist for the use of Benedictine missionaries among the Saxon tribes of Germany. In his *De corpore et sanguine Domini,* Paschasius insisted that the body of Christ present in the Eucharist is the self-same body of Mary. As an antiphon set to music by numerous later composers in the Church would put it, in laudatory acclamation of this identity: *Ave verum corpus, natum de Maria Virgine,* 'Hail true body, born of Mary the Virgin'.[1] The relation between the Lord's eucharistic body and his historical (and so biological) body is one not simply of continuity but of essential sameness. Paschasius considers the objection that when Christ instituted the Eucharist at the Last Supper he had not yet suffered and died. The eucharistic body could not, therefore, be his historical body. He responds in the manner of all adroit controversialists. Rather than answering the question in its own terms, he confronts the objector with a problem inherent in the contrary position. Had Christ waited until after the Resurrection to give himself in the Eucharist in bodily form

> the heretics would have said that Christ is now incorruptible and located in heaven and that therefore his flesh cannot be eaten on earth by the faithful.[2]

Paschasius' sources were the realist passages about the presence in the Fathers. But precisely because of his rich patristic culture, typical of the Carolingian 'rebirth of studies', he was also acutely aware of the symbolist passages also. How could the Fathers simultaneously call the Eucharist *veritas,* 'reality', and *figura,* 'a figure'? Paschasius explains that the Eucharist is both figure and reality: while its appearance is bread and wine, its truth is the presence of Christ's body and blood, even though these are received in the sacrament by faith. For Paschasius, the real presence is absolutely indispensable for the function of this sacrament, which is to unite believers with the God-man in his very reality. Though Paschasius wisely rejected the notion that the Lord's body and blood were actually digested like ordinary food, individual phrases in his treatise were open to misunderstanding in that offensive way. Moreover, he would have had some difficulty in avoiding this danger completely, since he seems to have held that only by a miracle affecting the normal working of our senses do we not see on the altar the physical humanity of the Word, God, in this manner, graciously preventing us from being overwhelmed by the Eucharist's awesome greatness.

When in some few years' time his treatise was presented to the Carolingian emperor Charles the Bald, its ultra-realist account of the eucharistic presence gained it a mixed reception among the court intelligentsia. Another black monk theologian, Ratramnus, wrote a reply which centred on two questions. First, do the faithful receive the body and blood of Christ 'in a mystery', *in mysterio*, or 'in very truth', *in veritate*?[3] Secondly, is this the same body and blood as that which Mary bore? According to Ratramnus, the Eucharist is, in terms of the contrast he himself has posed, a 'mystery' that is, on his own definition:

> an action which exhibits one thing outwardly to the human senses and proclaims another thing inwardly to the minds of the faithful.[4]

Therefore, for him, it cannot be, in the alternative term of his couplet, 'truth', or what he calls:

> a representation of clear fact, not obscured by any shadowy images.[5]

Ratramnus' position has been summed up by saying that he believed the Eucharist to be in the order of practical reality what a metaphor is in the order of language — the expression of one reality by reference to another reality quite distinct from it. If we say that, for instance, Richard I of England was 'a lion for bravery', we are claiming that one reality — lion-ness, in one of its (presumably well-founded) attributes — was expressed in another reality quite distinct from itself, namely Richard Coeur de Lion. And just as through their leonine qualities lions have some relation to brave men, so — returning now to the Eucharist — the historical body of Jesus bears some relation (via, presumably, the spiritual reality of the glorified Christ) to the consecrated elements. That licenses us to call those elements 'the body and blood of Christ', but we must be candid in conceding the distinct autonomy of the two realities concerned. For Ratramnus, the consecrated elements are an enacted metaphor. They are an evocation in ritual of how the heavenly Christ feeds believers spiritually with his own life.

And this furnishes Ratramnus with the reply to his second question. The body of Christ which Mary bore cannot be that body of Christ which is present in the Eucharist. the first was an empirical body, made up of bones, nerves, flesh; the second is an interior spiritual reality expressed in an exterior physical sign. By interpreting the sometimes ambiguous evidence of the patristic tradition after his preferred fashion, Ratramnus came to conclusions much different from those of Paschasius.

Did Ratramnus simply deny the real presence? His repeated claim that, after the eucharistic consecration, 'no change has taken place',[6] may simply mean: no change that could — even in principle — be perceived by the senses. He set out to combat the Paschasian notion of a supernatural transformation of the bread and wine extending to their very appearances, veiled though this be to our sensory perception; in pruning back a theological excess, he cut too deep into the sap-bearing trunk of the Church's eucharistic faith.

Lanfranc and Berengar
A more satisfactory theology of the presence emerges in

the course of the eleventh century. Grit for the pearl was provided around 1040 by a French priest, Berengar (c.1010-1088), archdeacon of Tours, who revived Ratramnus' ideas in the new context of Aristotelian logic, the up-and-coming philosophical tool of the age. Berengar's contribution to eucharistic theology lay in obliging his critics to clarify their own view. Protected against hostile churchmen by his bishop, as well as his secular employer the Count of Anjou, Berengar found the Papacy more accommodating — at any rate at first. Pope Leo IX, the first of the great reforming popes from north of the Alps, attempted to arrange a public debate to discuss the issues, but this initiative was vetoed by the French king. The pope, accordingly, offered as an interim measure a simple compromise formula drawn up by Berengar himself. In 1059, however, the new Pope Nicholas II, under pressure from Norman theologians who considered Berengar little less than an heresiarch in the making, allowed his legate, Humbert of Silva Candida — whose intemperate excommunication of the Byzantine patriarch Michael Kerullarios had just precipitated *an* if not *the* Eastern schism — to impose on Berengar a quite draconian oath which revived Paschasius' ultra-realism in its sharpest form.

> The bread and wine which are laid on the altar [so the oath ran] are after the consecration not only a sacrament. They are also the true body and blood of our Lord Jesus Christ, and they are physically taken up and broken in the hands of the priest and crushed by the teeth of the faithful not only sacramentally but in truth.[7]

This formula, a source of some embarrassment to orthodox divines since, was based on an eighth-century gloss on the text of Augustine's homilies on the Gospel of St John. In his comments on John 6, Augustine had volunteered the judgement that 'the man who is not in Christ and Christ in him' certainly does not eat his flesh and drink his blood. To this the glossator added:

even if he physically and visibly crush with his teeth the sacrament of the body and blood of Christ.

The gloss could claim a certain exegetical foundation for its language. John's verb here for 'to eat', *trogein*, is exceptionally realistic (and might be translated 'to crunch'). But what is crushed according to the gloss are the sacramental elements, whereas in the oath it is Christ's body itself. Understandably unhappy with the outcome, Berengar repudiated the oath on return to France from Rome, though giving as reason its being taken under duress.

On Pope Nicholas' death in 1061 his successor, Alexander II, showed no interest in Berengar's case, but in 1063 the latter was confronted by a new adversary. This was Abbot Lanfranc of Bec, later to be Archbishop of Canterbury.[8] Although Lanfranc took the title of Paschasius' treatise as his own, his work showed a notable theological advance on his monastic predecessor. He found his cue in his study of Ambrose. In the *De sacramentis*, Ambrose had pointed out that if Christ, as the second person of the Holy Trinity, can create from nothing, then he must also have power to bring it about that

> things that do exist should continue in being or be changed into something else.[9]

In his comments on this text, Lanfranc proposed for the first time the idea of transubstantiation: the conversion of the substance, but not the accidents, of bread and wine, into the substance of Christ's being.

> The material objects on the Lord's Table which God sanctifies through the priest are — by the agency of God's power — indefinably, wondrously, in a way beyond our understanding, converted to the body of Christ in their being. Their outward appearances and certain other qualities remain unchanged, so that those who receive them are not shocked by the naked flesh and blood, and so that believers may receive the greater

rewards of faith. What we receive is the very body which was born of the Virgin, and yet it is not. It is, in respect of its being *(essentia)* and the characteristics and power of its true nature; it is not if you look at the outward appearance *(species)* of the bread and wine.[10]

Berengar's reply to Lanfranc, the *De sacra Coena*, was shrewd. For Lanfranc, or so Berengar maintained, the sacrament has ceased to be a sign, pointing beyond itself. By insisting that the visible forms of bread and wine are metaphysically combined with the invisible reality of Jesus Christ, Lanfranc had removed the Eucharist from the sacramental order.[11]

For a second time, the affair came to the ears of Church authority. In 1079 Pope Gregory VII, Hildebrand, under criticism for doctrinal laxity from the German episcopate, moved to act in the Berengar case. Summoned again to Rome, Berengar accepted, with some reluctance, a new oath, which included a vital phrase for the future in the words 'substantially converted'. It read:

> I, Berengar, believe with my heart and confess with my mouth that the bread and wine which are placed on the altar are changed in their substance *(substantialiter converti)* into the true flesh and blood of Jesus Christ, by the Holy Prayer and the words of our Redeemer. They are thus, after consecration, the true body of Christ, born of the Virgin Mary, which was offered, and hung on the Cross, for the salvation of the world, and which sits on the right hand of the Father, and the real blood of Christ, which was shed from his side — and they are this, not only by virtue of the sign and the power of this sacrament, but in their peculiar nature and their substantial reality.[12]

Berengar's difficulties with this second oath revolved around the crucial phrase 'substantially converted'. As to those words, by his own account, he could only sign with grave mental reservations. Professor Henry Chadwick has shown that Berengar remained obdurate in his conviction that to surrender belief in the natural reality of the bread and wine, after the consecratory prayer, is to lose access to the signs which give access to Christ's saving reality. This was a position which could claim some semblance of authority from Augustine; Berengar strengthened it by the logical consideration that to speak of 'consecrated bread and wine' must imply that bread and wine survive in being consecrated. Their consecration consists not in the passing away of their being but in its elevation 'to be something better', *in melius* — a phrase Berengar borrowed from Augustine on the Incarnation.[13]

> Sadly, he had found the pope weak, despite Gregory's expression of trust in Berengar's legitimate place within the Augustinian tradition and a vision in which the Blessed Virgin had instructed the pope not to require of Berengar any dogma going beyond authoritative *scripturae*.[14]

Berengar died edifyingly, as a hermit on an island in the Loire. Before leaving the Berengarian controversy, however, we should note two things. First, there is an ambivalence in his writings, or what remains of them, comparable to the difficulties which doctrinal historians have found in the assessment of Ratramnus. Sometimes he affirms a real presence of Christ, while denying that this involves the outright conversion of the elements into Christ's body and blood — this will be, later, the moderate Reformation position of Luther. At other times, he anticipates such 'left-wing' Reformation teaching as that of Zwingli, saying, in effect, that the consecrated elements are only tokens. Secondly, Berengar's opponents manifest this ambivalence in a mirror of their own. At times, they simply wish to affirm that the consecrated elements are truly identical with the Lord's being. But on other occasions, they ascribe to the suffering and glorified person of the Saviour in the Eucharist what can only be properly attributed to the sacramental species. Still, it is worth bearing in mind here the judicious comment of Darwell Stone:

> While there is no doubt [wrote the High Anglican historian of eucharistic doctrine] that carnal tendencies existed both in language and in thought, the probability must not be forgotten that such phrases as 'the real body and blood of our Lord Jesus Christ are held and broken by the hands of the priest and crushed by the teeth of the faithful' were used by many as clumsy ways of expressing the conviction that the sacrament which is held and broken and crushed is the body and blood of Christ.[15]

The careless formulation of the oath of 1059 would have an appeal in some unexpected quarters. Luther, attracted, no doubt, by language he found not so much clumsy as vigorous and earthy, praised the oath for its ruling out of a 'double manducation' — something unacceptably dualist in the Saxon Reformer's eyes. To feed on the elements physically by the body and on Christ spiritually by the soul is to divide what God, in creating us, and nourishing us with the holy sacrament, has united.

During the next century, the twelfth, the conviction settles over the theological community that the most appropriate term for the wonderful change which the elements, in the economies of the Son and the Spirit, undergo in the Liturgy is 'substantial conversion' or 'transubstantiation'. It is this conviction which the Fourth Lateran Council of 1215, convoked and ratified by Pope Innocent III, would express in its own eucharistic teaching.

> There is one universal Church of the faithful, outside which no one at all is in a state of salvation. In this Church, Jesus Christ himself is both priest and sacrifice; and his body and blood are really contained in the sacrament of the altar under the species of bread and wine, the bread being transubstantiated into the body,

and the wine into the blood, by the power of God,
so that, to effect the mystery of unity, we ourselves
receive of that which is his, what he himself received
of that which is ours.[16]

Chadwick has pointed out the touch of paradox in the
circumstance that this doctrine of a change of metaphysical
substance arose from the need to avert Humbert's
'materialistic and naturalistic interpretation of eucharistic
change and reception', so that the safeguarding, in Latin
Christendom, of a genuinely spiritual view of the Eucharist
fell to two popes — Gregory VII and Innocent III — who
have 'commonly enjoyed a distinguished place in Protestant
demonology and myth'.[17] We shall not be far wrong in finding
additionally in these words a plea to separated Western
Christians to find in the dogma of transubstantiation an
equilibrium and repose amidst the clashing possibilities which
eucharistic thinking has engendered.

The theology of Thomas

The classic account of that dogma in Latin Christian thought
awaits us in questions 73 to 78 of the *tertia pars* of Thomas'
Summa Theologiae. From what we have seen of the Paschasian
and Berengarian controversies, it will not surprise us to
discover that Thomas opens his discussion of the presence
by asking whether Christ's body is in this sacrament *secundum
veritatem*, 'really and truly', or only *secundum figuram*, 'in a
figurative way'. Citing various Church Fathers, Thomas opts
for the former, since, as he remarks, such a 'real' presence
fits more appropriately with the New Covenant, with the
'perfection' (as he calls it) of the Christian dispensation.[18]
And he offers a reasoned justification for why this is so.

First, the Old Testament already had a figurative
expression of the Passion of Christ. Its ritual sacrifices
prefigured the death of the true Lamb. Rightly, then, the
sacrifice of the New Law instituted by Christ should have
aliquid plus, 'something more', than that. Appropriately, it

contains Christ himself who suffered for us, and that not merely in a token (*significatio*) but in actual reality as well. Secondly, such a real presence, Thomas argues, better befits the charity of Christ which led him to take a human body for our sakes at the Incarnation. It is in the highest degree proper to friendship, Thomas explains, that friends should live together. They should share that common life which bodily communication makes possible. In heaven, we shall see Christ, the King, in his beauty; but even here on our pilgrimage, he has not left us without his bodily presence. So Thomas calls this sacrament since it joins Christ and ourselves so intimately, *signum maximae caritatis*, 'the sign of the greatest possible charity', and *nostrae spei sublevamentum*, the 'arousal of our hope'. Thirdly, for Christ to be really present in his body and blood is more appropriate to the nature of Christian faith which bears not only on Christ's Godhead but also on his manhood. The divine Word in whom we put our faith is also the human Jesus, for Jesus' embodied humanity is the 'conjoined instrument' of the Word in our salvation.

Probably by coincidence, Thomas touches on Berengar's weightiest objection to eucharistic realism: by denying that Christ is present symbolically in the Eucharist do we not remove it from the order of signs, and so overthrow its nature as a sacrament? Thomas replies, in effect, that signs may have different ways of signifying, diverse modes in which they act as signs. The sacramental signs at large already differ from natural signs because they effect or bring about what they represent. In the Eucharist we have something else again: Christ is present there in the mode proper to this unique sacrament, which is a sign that not only brings about what it represents but also contains it.

Granted, then, that the body of Christ is truly present in this sacrament, do the substances of bread and wine also endure there after the consecration?[19] The word 'substance' in this context had come down to Thomas, as we have seen, from the dogmatic tradition — Lanfranc to Lateran IV. It was also familiar to his readers from the philosophy they had studied in the liberal arts courses of the mediaeval schools. But for us today, a word about its import is desirable.

Thomas possesses a rich philosophical vocabulary for describing, or analysing, the concrete structure of reality, the way things are. Three of the most important key words are: *esse, substantia* and *accidentia. Accidents* for mediaeval philosophy are not, evidently, what we mean in everyday speech today: events in the human world not willed by any human agent, like a child catching rabies, or King's Cross underground station catching fire. For Thomas, accidents are those aspects of reality which require for their existence a created ground which is other than themselves. Thus, while the redness of a red apple certainly exists, it only exists by inhering in the apple itself. Accidents are features of reality that have no visible means of support unless they find it in some other aspect of reality which has the ontological solidity that they lack. And this second aspect of reality Thomas calls *substance*. Substance is a concrete reality in so far as it needs no other created ground than itself. The desk on which I am writing is substantial because it is not parasitic on any other concrete reality for its existence. It does not inhere in anything, though something — for instance, oblong-shapedness, hardness, brownness — inheres in it. It is typical of substances, according to Thomas, that they enjoy a certain autonomy, independence or self-sufficiency within the created order. However, such autonomy is only relative, for ultimately, just as accidents require grounding in substance, so substance requires grounding in *esse*, usually translated the 'act of being'. Precisely by virtue of being created, the world, composed as it is of substances with their accidents, is a world which only endures because it constantly receives being. God who is infinite actuality, *actus purus*, communicates being, the act of being, to creatures as the deepest foundation of their existence. So as to draw attention to the fact that substances with their accidents are dependent for their own ground on God, Thomas describes them as *entia*, 'be-ings', from the verbal participle of *esse, ens*: finite participations in the infinite *esse* or act of being which God, as Creator, is.

In actual experience, the order in which we come to grasp reality follows the sequence in which I have treated these topics: first accidents, then substances, finally being. What we encounter in the world is, in the first place, the myriad forms of what is seen, heard, touched, tested, but through this sensuous richness and variety the human mind discerns the ordered inter-relation of substances which ground these accidents. The mind discovers intelligible patterns in the world, patterns which coincide with distinct concrete things, and enable them to possess significance in their own right. Through crustiness, doughiness, crispy–brownness or sometimes flabby whiteness I find bread: my intelligence meets an intelligibility which corresponds to the mind's most natural question, What is it? Only by reflecting rationally on the conditions of possibility for such substances, presented to me through their accidents, do I reach the third stage, the stage of *esse*, by asking how it is possible for something which does not have within it its own ground of being to exist.

Well, then, do the substances of bread and wine remain in this sacrament after the consecration? Thomas replies that such co-existence of Christ's real presence with the substances of bread and wine is impossible. He argues that Christ's body can only come to be in this sacrament by one of two ways. Either it is brought in from outside, or something already there is changed into it. But there can be no question of Christ's body moving through space: among many difficulties, this would entail that body ceasing to be in heaven.[20] This leaves only the possibility that the substance of bread changes into it: and this explains why Christ said not 'Here is my body' but 'This is my body', for the latter proposition would be false were the substance of bread still present. Moreover, the worship the Church gives this sacrament would be altogether misguided if the consecrated elements contained a created substance which ought not to receive adoration.

This change (*conversio*) of the substance of bread into the substance of Christ's body must be counted *omnino supernaturalis*, 'entirely beyond the powers of nature'.[21] It is brought about sheerly through the power of God. Unlike God, a created agent, such as ourselves, or an earthquake, has only a limited range of action. A created agent can change reality only in the sense of changing the form of some reality: the distinctive organisation of matter which makes something an intelligible kind of something with characteristic capacities, whether active or passive. Such a 'formal change' is not what happens in the eucharistic conversion. To have some inkling of what does happen there, we must remember that God is infinite actuality and that, accordingly, his action extends, as Thomas puts it, 'to the whole being of a thing'. God is able to bring about a *conversio totius entis*, a transformation of the way it participates in *esse* so as to be this individual substance and not that.

> The author of being is able to change that which is being in the one into that which is being in the other by taking away what kept this from being that.[22]

Since such a change is unique, we give it a name all its own: *transubstantiatio*.

For St Thomas, the moment when this real presence is achieved in the offerings of the Church comes when the words of institution of the Eucharist, as given in the Gospels from the lips of Christ, are repeated, in the liturgical drama, by the celebrating priest.[23] For some students of the history of the liturgy, Thomas' clear-cut position on this point (he remarks that the rest of the canon of the Mass is unnecessary for the consecration, though a celebrant who omitted all else would sin gravely in failing to observe the rite of the Church) derives from the internal demands of the doctrine of transubstantiation itself. Transubstantiation, it may be said, entails an instantaneous transformation of the gifts. On the other hand, Aquinas may well have been reacting to the somewhat confused and implausible alternative positions taken up by a number of his predecessors: Amalarius of Metz, for example, seems to have considered that the Our Father could consecrate, while the prayer of the Roman liturgy at the Fraction, 'This commingling *and consecration*' may have given rise to misunderstandings in others.[24] Still, though Thomas did not advert to the importance of the *epiklêsis* in the East, or of the *epiklêsis*-like prayers in the Roman liturgy of his day, he by no means neglected the role of the Holy Spirit in the consecration.[25] Interpreting Augustine, he insists that for the body of Christ to be present in the Eucharist 'spiritually' does not mean in 'mystical signification' alone, but rather 'invisibly and through the power of the Spirit'.[26] A little later in his treatment of the presence in the *Summa Theologiae*, he stresses that, at the consecration, bread is changed into Christ's body 'by the power of the Spirit alone'.[27] Perhaps the best adjudication of the whole consecration question, so controverted in later Catholic-Orthodox polemic, is to say that the eucharistic transformation takes place at the words of institution (the Latin stress) but not as in any way separated from their context in the entire eucharistic prayer which should itself be regarded as 'epicletic' in character (so picking up the Greek emphasis).[28]

The way in which Christ exists in this sacrament as a result of this 'wonderful conversion' is grasped only by the uncreated mind of God. But, Thomas thinks, the glorified minds of angels and of human beings can come to some understanding of it in heaven through a sharing in God's own knowledge of himself. For *homo viator*, man on pilgrimage, by contrast, it can be known only through faith, on the authority of the Word of God revealing.[29] Thomas rarely, if ever, calls the conversion a miracle. Its closest analogy lies not with miracles but with the act of creation. Bringing the body of Christ out of bread should be compared to the original creative act bringing being out of non-being, rather than to a modification of the laws of nature. What can be called miraculous, however, is the way in which God preserves the accidents of bread and wine in being even when the substance in which they inhered is no longer present.[30] For the accidents are really present in the Eucharist, just as is the substance of Christ's body. Some of Thomas' contemporaries wondered whether the accidents were truly there: a hang-over from the ultra-realism of Paschasius and Humbert. Thomas has to deal with an objector who maintains that the accidents do not genuinely nourish but only refresh by bringing about a change of feeling in the recipient, as when a person feels stronger from the very smell of food or euphoric at the smell of wine. But Thomas gives them the same active characteristic which bread and wine everywhere possess: were a man to consume a large quantity of consecrated hosts, he remarks, robustly, he could be kept going nutritionally for a long time.[31]

Finally Thomas raises and answers one or two other important matters handed down on the agenda of the past. First of all, what is meant by calling the blessed sacrament *corpus Christi,* the *body* of Christ? Though using the phrase 'the body of Christ' for the sacrament, Thomas insists that we have to do here with *totus Christus,* 'the whole Christ' — not in Augustine's sense of that phrase, the head with his members, but in the sense of Christ's total being, divinity and humanity.[32] While, as a result of the sacramental sign, Christ's body and blood are present as the 'term of the conversion', nevertheless they cannot in reality be separated from Christ's soul and his Godhead. It is only by an act of our minds that we distinguish these realities that are actually found together. Thomas provides a convenient phrase for this state of affairs: presence 'by natural concomitance'. It follows that the whole Christ is found under either species.

Moreover, he is present under each and every part of the appearances of bread and wine. The dimensions of Christ's body are in this sacrament not in the way that is normal for dimensions to be, but in the way that is natural for substance to be, and the whole nature of any substance is given to us under any part of the dimensions that contain it.[33] The whole nature of bread is in a crumb, as in a loaf. For Thomas, our Lord is not present 'locally' in his sacrament. He does not occupy the space taken up by its species; he does not move when the species are elevated liturgically in the Mass, or carried in a pyx to the sick, or raised processionally in the monstrance on the feast of Corpus Christi.

Nor is he directly subject in the sacrament to any other kind of change. When the species cease to be, the body of Christ ceases to be under them, not because the body of Christ in any way depends on them, but because the relation between the body of Christ and the species has ceased to be.[35] In the same way, Thomas observes, God ceases to be the Lord of some created thing when that thing has ceased to exist: the change takes place not in God but in the creature. The Lord's body, being glorified, is beyond all change, or anything that we may do to it. The fraction — *pace* the first oath imposed on Berengar — takes place in the accidents alone. Yet, since the sacramental species are the sign of the real body of Christ so their fraction is the sign of our Lord's Passion which he endured in his broken body on Golgotha.[36]

What, in conclusion, may be the status of the language of transubstantiation today? In a famous phrase, the Council of Trent called the word a 'most appropriate' one for this wonderful change,[37] and that comment has suggested to some a willingness on the Council's part to leave open the door for other hopeful candidates to enter. Whether as a matter of historical fact this is so may be doubted, for the Council made the idiom its own in describing the conversions taking place *vere, realiter, substantialiter*.[38] Nevertheless, it is true that, in principle, a Council's formulations of the Church's faith may be transposed into other conceptualities if they can be or need be. It can be argued, though, that the metaphysical analysis found in the concept of transubstantiation derives from questions about the world so fundamental that they are pervasive in every culture, and built into the fabric of human rationality itself. No one is rational who cannot ask, What is it? or see the meaning of that question. All of this leaves untouched, however, the *purpose* of the real presence, which is addressed in chapter 4.

4

The Mediaevals on the Purpose of the Real Presence

In the last chapter, we looked at the development of the doctrine of the eucharistic presence in the Western Church, up to and including St Thomas. We saw that the early mediaeval Church made a decisive option for a realist conception of the presence, according to which, 'by a wonderful change' the consecrated bread and wine are converted into the personal being of Jesus Christ. We found subsequently that the classic account of what that 'conversion' involves is found in Thomas, who presents it in terms of a metaphysical exploration of being. Such an exploration is necessary if we are to make reasonable sense of what the Church does in her liturgical cultus.

In this chapter I look at the *purpose* of that real presence. Maintaining the historical approach to doctrine which has characterised this book from the outset, I consider the purpose of the presence in terms of those theologians who first gave us a clear formulation of the doctrine of the real presence: namely, the early mediaevals with Thomas at their crowning close.

Fundamentally, mediaeval theology knows of two rationales for the first presence: the union of believers with Christ, and their union with each other in the Church. At root, these two notions of the aim of eucharistic participation can already be found in Paul's Corinthian correspondence. But now they are described more reflectively, and even systematically. I shall call them the 'mystical' and the 'ecclesial' rationales of the presence.[1]

The mystical rationale
Firstly, then, how did mediaeval theologians understand the mystical rationale: the eucharistic presence as joining us with

Christ and, through him, with the mystery of the triune God? The mediaevals envisaged holy communion in the context of the Incarnation.[2] They took it for granted that the Incarnation was God's greatest work, the uniting of humanity to himself in the person of his Son. Relating this to the Eucharist, the twelfth-century writer, Honorius of Autun, holds that Christ took on human nature, so that, through the reception of his flesh in the Eucharist, we might be joined to him, and through this union be joined to the Godhead itself.[3] This conviction led Honorius' contemporary, Rupert of Deutz, to argue that sacramental reception is necessary for salvation — an idea still current in the time of St Thomas.[4] Thomas will deal with it by identifying a sense in which this is true. Because the Eucharist is the centre and climax of the sacramental life, to which baptism is the entrance, the desire for baptism — itself certainly necessary for salvation — is implicitly a desire for the Eucharist to which baptism gives access.[5] Yet mediaeval theologians were quite aware that the simple reception of the elements does not in itself guarantee union with Christ, and so with the Father. They distinguished, indeed, between a reception which was simply *corporeale*, 'bodily', and one which was truly *spirituale*, 'spiritual'. Proper reception of the elements entails having the right dispositions. How those dispositions should be described varies from one author to another. Lanfranc has it that only those who, in receiving communion, recall the Passion of Christ, and imitate the crucified Christ by charity and purity of heart, actually receive unto salvation, and his view, in its admirable evangelical spirit, may perhaps be allowed to do service for a multitude of others.[6] But would this mean then, people asked, that unless we have such positive dispositions the sacrament will do us no good? Has sacramental reception no power to create right dispositions in us, at least if we do not oppose its working? By the time of Thomas theologians will nuance this point. For St Thomas, communion always brings grace to us so long as we present no obstacle to its grace in our communicating. But the fruitfulness of that grace in our lives turns on our own spiritual dispositions.[7]

The mediaevals described the mystical rationale — like its complement, the ecclesial rationale, still to be considered — as the *res* of the Eucharist. Literally translated, this means the Eucharist's 'thing', but the word can be helpfully paraphrased in a number of ways, of which the most important for our purposes are, in different contexts, the Eucharist's 'further reality' or 'ultimate purpose'. According to the mediaeval analysis, the species of bread and wine are themselves the sign of a *res*, namely, the body and blood of Christ, and, by 'natural concomitance', of the entire personal being of Jesus Christ as both man and God. But while in relation to the sacramental species, this body and blood of the Saviour is *res* — the further reality which the signs signify — nevertheless, the gift of the Lord's body and blood can itself be said, in a second movement of thought, to possess a *res*, and not just to be one. The *res* of Christ's eucharistic presence, its further reality in the sense of its ultimate purpose, is our incorporation into Christ through faith, hope and charity. The mediaevals distinguished, therefore, between the reality embodied in the sacramental sign and its ultimate goal. They made a distinction between, first, the further reality present sacramentally via the symbol, or the accidents, and this they called *res et sacramentum*: literally, the 'thing and the sacrament', a phrase we might render as 'the sacramental reality', and secondly, the ultimate reality or purpose of the sacrament, why the sacrament is there at all, which they termed either *res sacramenti*, literally 'the thing of the sacrament', to be paraphrased as 'the purpose for which the sacramental reality is given', or, more simply, just *res* without any qualification': the ultimate purpose or reality *tout court*.[8]

Many spiritual theologians of the period, and notably in the school of Laôn, in northern France, and the Parisian abbey of St Victor, stressed the decisive importance of the ultimate *res* of the presence which, in the context of the mystical rationale of the real presence, will mean our union with God in Christ. For this reason, they regarded what became known as 'spiritual communion' as something equivalent in significance to a worthy reception of the sacramental species. If one cannot receive the outward sign of the Eucharist, then contrition and charity can suffice to gain, during the Liturgy, the spiritual union with Christ at which the Eucharist aims.[9] This remains an important point in the pastoral care of people in irregular marital situations or of others who, for whatever reason, are sacramentally excommunicate. In the Middle Ages themselves, however, the most frequent ground for not receiving sacramentally was, surely, awe before the eucharistic presence, an attitude which the triumph of the sacramental realists both presupposed and fostered. Although there was a strong social pressure to receive communion on the great feasts, this was matched by an equally powerful fear of approaching Christ unworthily. Confessors did not just expect a person to be free from mortal sin. More than this, a would-be communicant should have a true longing for union with Christ, evidenced in carrying out acts of penance and of charity. Some theologians actively discouraged frequent reception on the grounds that familiarity with the sacrament would breed indifference. This is a more cogent objection to frequent communion than that proposed in the seventeenth century by Catholics affected by Jansenist rigorism. According to the latter, it is extremely difficult, in the Christian life, not to be in a state of mortal sin. Such a theology of grace (or its absence) offered a very different argument against frequent communicating from the mediaeval one, which is essentially prudential, concerned with the practical possibility of trivialising the sacrament. St Thomas has a characteristically sane and balanced discussion of the point which is worth citing in full. He writes:

> Two considerations about the reception of this sacrament. The first regards the sacrament itself, the

virtue of which is salutary to man: consequently, it is profitable to receive daily, so as to gather its fruits daily. Hence Ambrose says, 'if whenever Christ's blood is shed, it is shed for the forgiveness of sins, I, who sin often, should receive it often; I need a frequent remedy'. The second (consideration) regards the recipient, who is required to approach this sacrament with great reverence and devotion. Consequently, if someone finds he has these dispositions every day, he does well to receive daily.[10]

Thomas qualifies this assertion at once, however, by way of a reference to St Augustine.

Augustine, after saying, 'Receive daily that it may profit you daily', adds, 'So live as to deserve to receive it daily'. Since many are often impeded from such devotion, on account of indispositions of body and soul, it is not expedient for all to approach this sacrament daily, but as often as they find themselves properly prepared. So we are told, 'Neither praise nor blame daily reception of the Eucharist'.[11]

And yet, if one's lack of appropriate dispositions could rightly hold one back from sacramental communion, the same, presumably, could be said in relation to spiritual communion with the sacramentally present Christ. William of Auxerre was, apparently, the first of many thirteenth-century theologians to enquire whether someone in mortal sin might, without further sin, view the host at the moment of its liturgical lifting up at the consecration.[12]

St Thomas' summary of the preceding tradition strikes a more positive note. To consider the effect of this sacrament, he advises us to look at *quod in hoc (sacramento) continetur*, 'what it holds', and this is Christ. Making explicit the parallel with the Incarnation, he comments:

Just as by coming visibly into the world he brought the life of grace into it, so by coming to men sacramentally he causes the life of grace.[13]

Secondly, attend to *quod per hoc sacramentum repraesentatur*, 'what is represented by this sacrament', and this is the Passion of Christ. The fruits that Christ's Passion wrought on the Cross are bestowed, in dependence on the events of Calvary, upon the individual person by this sacrament of the sacrifice of Christ. Thirdly, Thomas writes, study the *modus quo traditur hoc sacramentum*, 'the manner of this sacrament's giving', namely, food and drink. Evidently, this sacrament does for the life of the spirit what material food and drink produce for the life of the body: sustaining, building up, restoring, contenting. Having pondered these three aspects of holy communion, we can only conclude that the *res sacramenti*, the ultimate purpose and reality of this sacrament, is the grace of union with Christ. For this reason, Thomas calls every reception of the Eucharist *viaticum* (and not merely one's last holy communion, at the hour of death) because what this sacrament gives us is the power to reach glory, the vision of God.

Nor does Thomas exclude the possibility that holy communion brings about in our lives the necessary negative preparation for this consummation: the forgiveness of sins. With respect to the forgiving of mortal sin (which has its own sacraments in baptism and penance), he is properly guarded. Someone who receives the blessed sacrament whilst conscious of mortal sin cannot find in communion the means of reconciliation with the holy God. Thomas' argument as to why such a person is not a fit recipient of the Eucharist is properly doctrinal and not moralistic.[14] First, such a believer is not spiritually alive — and yet, to receive the spiritual nourishment this sacrament brings one must be spiritually alive. Secondly, for as long as a person keeps his attachment to mortal sin, his affection for it, he cannot be united with Christ, which union is, however, the true *res* of the sacrament. Nonetheless, St Thomas does allow that, in two restricted senses, the Eucharist does forgive even mortal sins. In the first place, a mortal sinner as yet outside the Church but preparing to enter it receives the gift of justification and is forgiven in the waters of baptism, precisely as a result of the implicit desire for this sacrament. Secondly, and this thought concerns those who are already members of the Church, the Eucharist forgives the mortal sins of those who are neither conscious of such sins, nor attached to them, and in that condition approach the sacrament.[15] By coming to communion with reverence and devotion, such a mortal sinner receives the grace of charity, which makes contrition complete and brings forgiveness. For venial sins, on the other hand, the Eucharist is consistent forgiveness. As Thomas explains:

> The body needs nourishment to restore what is lost daily through the action of natural heat. In the life of the soul, too, something is lost in us every day through venial sin which lessens the warmth of charity. But the Eucharist confers the virtue of charity, because it is the sacrament of love.[16]

To understand the eucharistic presence in terms of the mystical rationale, is, evidently, to see it as the 'antepast of heaven': a theme of patristic piety and reflection touched on in chapter 2. St Thomas, in composing new texts for the feast of Corpus Christi, enhanced the already considerable capacity of the prayers of the Roman rite (and notably those said after Communion) to portray the Eucharist as a foretaste of the banquet of the Kingdom. The Eucharist is the pledge, *pignus*, of heaven. As Thomas puts it, acclaiming this sacrament in his antiphon for the Magnificat at the Vesper office of Corpus Christi:

> O sacred banquet in which Christ is received, the memory of his passion cultivated, the heart filled with grace, and the pledge of future glory given us!

In these matters, St Thomas' principal concern lies with the Eucharist and *personal* eschatology: the final condition of the Christian in the full blossoming of friendship with God. And yet, as Aquinas' eucharistic sequence, the *Lauda*

Sion, whole-heartedly recognises, if the Eucharist is the antepast of heaven, and first-fruits of the Kingdom, then it must be, of its nature, a communal reality — since heaven and the Kingdom are, for the imagery of Scripture and Tradition, the *social* co-presence of human beings to God.[17]

The ecclesial rationale

It is time, then, to move on to the second principal account of the purpose of the real presence, its ecclesial rationale. So far little has been said in this context about the Eucharist as a banquet which at once celebrates and creates the unity of Christians within a single sacred community. But in a complementary tradition to the one considered so far, Gilbert de la Porrée could describe the *res sacramenti* of the Eucharist not so much as a personal bond with Christ, but as that multi-ply, inter-personal bond of all the redeemed which is the Church.[18] As we saw in the case of Augustine's theology, the 'power' of the Eucharist is unity. For Augustine, since the eucharistic presence has as its rationale the uniting of believers to each other through their union with Christ, so we become his ecclesial body through feeding on the eucharistic body of Christ. In direct or indirect dependence on the African doctor, Latin Christian writers at the turn of the patristic and the mediaeval age see the relation of Eucharist to Church as one of cause and effect, means and end, sign and reality. The same *perichorêsis*, or mutual indwelling, of Church and Eucharist expressed in Augustine's sermons crops up in a whole host of authors stretching from Ildephonsus of Toledo, Isidore of Seville and Gregory of Elvira in sub-Roman Spain, to Jonas of Orleans, Florus of Lyons and Walafrid Strabo in Frankish Gaul.[19] The eucharistic assembly, as Cardinal Henri de Lubac showed in his study, *Corpus mysticum* — for which he chose as sub-title 'The Eucharist and the Church in the Middle Ages' — is a mystery of communion, simultaneously eucharistic and ecclesial in character. In the late patristic and early mediaeval West, the word 'communion' denotes, according to the context, both reception of the sacrament and union with the Church. For the theologians of the empire of Charlemagne, for example, the 'sanctorum communio' (communion of saints) of the Apostles' Creed was at once communion with the glorified dead and communion in the Church — through common participation in the Eucharist.[20]

Returning to the high Middle Ages with which this section opened: later theologians belonging to Gilbert de la Porrée's school are frank in describing the Eucharist as, in its deepest reality, a sign of salvific membership in the Church. Gerhoh of Reichersberg, for example, distinguishes between the *signa* of the Eucharist (the sacramental species), its *essentia* (the being of Christ, present through those signs), and the *res sacramenti* — which is, for Gerhoh, not so much the redeeming body of the Lord as his redeemed body, the Church. Accepting gratefully a phrase of Augustine's, Gerhoh declares the Eucharist to be a 'sacrament of unity', and understands this of the unity of the Church. Accordingly, Gerhoh denies that the *res sacramenti* of the Eucharist can be found outside the visible communion of the Catholic Church. Beyond the boundaries of the unity it represents, the sacrament of unity can have no meaning, no effect. Indeed, salvation consists in the 'worthy participation of the faithful in the sacraments, and their persevering in unity by means of them'.[21]

These ideas are modified by the school of Peter Abelard.[22] In the view of some modern students, the Abelardians feared that the ecclesial rationale of the real presence, should it come to be defined *over against* the mystical rationale, would finish by eliminating altogether any explicit reference to Christ in an account of the Eucharist's ultimate significance. They insisted, therefore, that the *res sacramenti* of the Eucharist must be the union not only of the members, but of Head and members, in the Church. Dr Gary Macy has pointed out that this ecclesial rationale of the eucharistic presence is, at one level, an inference from the very structure of the eucharistic liturgy itself.

The reception of the sacrament at Christmas, Pentecost and especially Easter was a dramatic and physically obvious witness to the unity of the Church. All members in good standing appeared in their parish churches, hopefully cleansed from sin, ready to partake of the effective sign of the community of the sacred, and to pay the dues which their membership required.[23]

Such an ecclesiological account of the purpose of the real presence — the unification of the Church, Head and members — passed into general currency through the work of Peter Lombard whose *Sentences* were the main textbook of theological students in the West until (in some places, well after) the Reformation. For Lombard, the *res sacramenti* is the union of the predestined, those who will make up the glorified Church in heaven. But increasingly, and above all with St Thomas, the term used is *corpus mysticum Christi*, 'Christ's mystical body'.[24] The sacramental bread and wine bring about the presence of Christ, human and divine, in the body he took from Mary, suffered in upon the Cross, and rose with at Easter. But this personal body is itself the medium of a more extensive reality, the whole Christ in Augustine's sense: Christ and ourselves, united in the Kingdom of which the visible Church is itself the primordial sacrament. In this formulation, the 'vertical' concern of the 'mystical rationale' writers, and the 'horizontal' concern of their 'ecclesial rationale' colleagues find simultaneous expression.

Although such 'eucharistic ecclesiology' was not the dominant choice of the high Middle Ages, for Thomas too there is a relation between the Eucharist and the *corpus Ecclesiae*, the 'body of the Church'. In his understanding, the sacraments do not simply illustrate the grace which flows from the mysteries of the life of Christ — above all, those which constitute the Paschal mystery of his death and resurrection. More than this, the sacraments prolong, through their work of signifying, the action of the 'cause' — the historic event in the life of the incarnate Word — to which the Christian will be assimilated by grace. And this is most importantly true of the Eucharist in its relation to the death and resurrection of Christ, and to the pentecostal outpouring of the Holy Spirit. In the sacramental effects of the eucharistic Bread and Wine, these central mysteries of the world's salvation endure, with all their efficacy intact. In the Eucharist, the Word, with the Holy Spirit, continues to bring about those ends for which the Incarnation and the Atonement happened. And this he does precisely by forming the body of the Church.

To speak at all of the 'ecclesial rationale' of the real presence is, of course, to advert to the inter-connection of two themes which have been with us since the patristic period, and, indeed, since Paul: the Eucharist as presence, and as foundation of the Church. But if, for some, at any rate, of the high mediaeval theologians, the motifs of the presence and the Church's foundation were securely inter-bound, less has been said about the fate of the third of the patristic trio of themes: the Eucharist as sacrifice. It is to that theme, in resuming the story-line, that we now turn.

5

The Eucharistic Sacrifice from Trent to the Nineteenth Century

We left the theme of the eucharistic sacrifice in the patristic period. We saw that the Fathers spoke of the entire Christian life as a spiritual sacrifice, but were also willing to use the word 'sacrifice' in a heightened sense for the Eucharist. They took it that the eucharistic action enjoys a special relationship both with the sacrifice of Calvary and with the abiding heavenly sacrifice of Jesus Christ. In heaven, Christ offers his sacred humanity to the Father in a continuous gesture of obedient love, in this way interceding for the Church and the world. Lastly, we found that, with Augustine, a reflective theology of the eucharistic sacrifice appears on the stage of Christian thought for the first time. St Augustine regarded the eucharistic action as our sacramental insertion into the sacrifice of the Mediator. The Church, Christ's body, co-offers the sacrifice of her Head, thus learning to make his sacrifice her own.

Towards Trent: the making of an agenda

In the Middle Ages, the development of the doctrine of eucharistic sacrifice was chiefly implicit, rather than explicit. It was implied in a developing sense of the Eucharist as what the Council of Trent would later call 'a true and proper sacrifice'. The symptomatic manifestations of this sense were found in art, in devotional habits, and the literature which supported them, and in such institutions as foundation Masses, chantry chapels, and the system of Mass stipends. To a much lesser extent was there development of explicit doctrine, at the level of theology — perhaps just because the centre of attention was occupied by the theme discussed in the last two chapters, the real presence. In terms of formal theologising, the motif of the real sacrifice fell into the background. In Thomas' *Summa Theologiae*, for example, out of eighty-two articles devoted to the Eucharist, only two are consecrated explicitly to the real sacrifice.[1] Thomas' way of introducing the theme of sacrifice is, however, of importance. He raises the issue by asking, Does this sacrament benefit others besides the recipients? In asking whether the eucharistic action brings any good to humankind beyond the limited number of those who actually celebrate it and receive the Holy Gifts in communion (whether sacramentally or only spiritually), we move beyond a consideration of the Eucharist as gift, presence and communion, and enter instead upon a discussion of the Eucharist as sacrifice.

The framework for mediaeval discussion of the eucharistic sacrifice was provided by Peter Lombard, who asked, Is what the priest does at the Eucharist properly called a sacrifice or immolation, and is Christ daily immolated, or was he immolated once only? He replies to his own question in these words:

> ... what is offered and consecrated by the priest is called a sacrifice and an immolation because it is a memorial and a representation of the true sacrifice and holy immolation made upon the altar of the Cross. Christ died once, upon the Cross, and there he was immolated in his own self; and yet every day he is immolated sacramentally, because in the sacrament there is a recalling of what was done once.[2]

This text raises a variety of questions which provide the agenda for the future of the theology of eucharistic sacrifice in our period. First, in what sense is the Eucharist, as a ritual action, the image of the bloody immolation of Calvary? What aspect of its ritual structure makes it such an image? Secondly, is the Eucharist merely the commemoration of a sacrifice, or is it a commemorative sacrifice? Is it, in other words, an action which commemorates a sacrifice in such a way that it is itself a sacrifice? And, if the latter, what may be the relation of the eucharistic sacrifice to the sacrifice of the Cross? Thirdly, how can he who is made present, Jesus Christ, be present precisely as the victim of his sacrifice, if in fact he is now glorious and impassible, able to suffer no more? Fourthly, if the agent of this sacramental sacrifice is the Church — first and foremost, the ministerial priesthood, and in the second place, the royal priesthood, the baptised who offer with the priest — does not this make of Christ a passive object who permits himself to be offered rather than actually performing the offering to the Father? Fifthly and lastly, what is the rationale, purpose or effect of this sacramental sacrifice?

By the time of the outbreak of the Protestant Reformation, Latin theology had come to a consensus on some of these issues whilst on others there was either discord of opinion or little or no discussion. The late mediaeval consensus may best be consulted in the work of Gabriel Biel of Tübingen, whose *Exposition of the Sacred Canon of the Mass* tried to collocate the best elements of the mediaeval theology of the sacrifice.[3] It was a treatise which Luther had studied thoroughly, having first read it with great fervour as a young monk preparing to celebrate his first Mass. He continued to regard it as the finest Catholic exposition of the Eucharist as sacrifice — a doctrine he himself came to denounce as 'the worst of all abuses', since it turned the Eucharist into a good work which Christians might perform as an active contribution to the salvation that, in reality, was wholly God's doing.[4] So far as our agenda of questions is concerned, on the first, Biel does not identify that aspect of the Mass-ritual which makes the Eucharist an image of Christ's sacrifice, but he is clear, *vis-à-vis* our second query, that the Mass, though a commemoration, is not a mere commemoration. In the Eucharist, the body and blood of Christ are not simply present as a gift to us. They are also present as an offering to the Father, under the appearances of bread and wine. This being so, the sacrifice of the altar is in a true sense one reality with the sacrifice of the Cross. The difference from the sacrifice of Calvary lies only in the manner of offering. For the Mass is a sacramental, bloodless sacrifice, whereas Calvary took place in a blood-stained fashion, in the order of natural existence, not in that of signs. This difference does not mean that the Mass is in some sense independent of the once-for-all sacrifice of the Cross: for Biel, the Eucharist was instituted (at the Last Supper) not as an 'absolute' but as a 'relative' or relational sacrifice: one which draws its significance and power, that is, from its relationship to the once-for-all death of the Redeemer. Next: Biel does not consider how Christ can be present as victim if now he enjoys a condition of glory, but on the fourth topic of the Lombard agenda, he does have something to contribute. To Biel's eyes, the fact that Christ constituted his followers as a holy priesthood, and instituted, within their sacred society, an order of ministerial priests to offer this sacrifice, others co-offering with them, shows that Christ is not passive in the Eucharist. Although he is truly offered by the Church, he himself enables such offering by granting the Church a share in his own High Priesthood. This he does in the sacraments of Baptism, Confirmation, and Order. Finally, the rationale of the eucharistic sacrifice, for Biel, consists in the mediation or application of the efficacy of the sacrifice of Calvary to human persons. The Eucharist is:

> a salutary and efficacious sign through which the salvation gained at such great cost should flow to the redeemed. . . . Whatsoever Christ our Saviour merited for men (liberation from evil, and bestowal of good, whether on earth, in purgatory or in heaven) when he offered himself on the Cross as a general redemption for all, is applied to each in particular through this sacrifice.[5]

Though Biel by no means answers all the questions which later theologians have put on the matter of the real sacrifice, the clarity and restraint of his doctrine is outstanding. It convicts of missing the mark those critics who decry the late mediaeval theology of the Mass as confused and superstitious, and thus attempt to explain, if not wholly to justify, the rejection of the sacrificial conception of the Eucharist by the Reformers. The most persistent accusation of the Reform against pre-Reformation theology, in this regard, was the claim that many unreformed Christians understood the sacrifice of Calvary as proptiation for original sin, and the eucharistic sacrifice as propitiation for personal sins, with the latter, then, taking on the form of an absolute sacrifice, one with effects obtained in its own right.[6] But Dr Francis Clark has shown that the evidence to support such a claim depends on a reading of only two texts, one from the Pseudo-Thomas and another from a contemporary, rather than a predecessor, of the Reformers, the Italian Dominican Ambrosius Catherinus, a *peritus* at the Council of Trent.[7] Even at the time, the Flemish theologian Albert Pighius could write of the polemical references to the Catholic theology of this subject in the Augsburg Confession:

> For very many years I have had experience of the Schools, which are open to all kinds of discussion and examination of the truth, and assertions about it, and I have never heard of or read of anyone advancing an opinion of this kind before I read their Confession... And even if they found such a person, they would have acted with less than candour in ascribing the stupidity of one man to us all.[8]

Trent itself may be said to have canonised the broad middle ground of the late mediaeval theology of the eucharistic sacrifice, more or less as represented by Biel. Here is how the Council fathers introduce the subject of the sacrifice of the Mass:

> Because his (Christ's) priesthood was not to end with his death, at the Last Supper, 'on the night when he was betrayed', in order to leave to his beloved Spouse,

the Church, a visible sacrifice — as the nature of man demands — by which the bloody sacrifice which he was once for all to accomplish on the Cross would be represented, its memory perpetuated until the end of the world and its salutary power applied for the forgiveness of the sins which we daily commit, declaring himself constituted 'a priest for ever after the order of Melchizedek', he (Christ) offered his body and blood under the species of bread and wine to God the Father, and, under the same signs, gave them to partake of the disciples, whom he then established as priests of the New Covenant, and ordered them and their successors in the priesthood to offer, saying, 'Do this as a memorial of me', as the Catholic Church has always understood and taught.[9]

The bishops at Trent go on to affirm that this visible sacramental sacrifice is truly propitiatory, for by it God grants grace and the gift of repentance, and pardons wrongdoing and sins, doing so not only for the living but also for those who have died in Christ but are not yet wholly purified.

Reflecting this latter doctrine, yet especially noteworthy for the manner of its formulation, is the third canon of the 1562 session of the Council, that devoted to the eucharistic sacrifice. For this canon insists on the need to affirm the overflow of the Eucharist's spiritual benefits to more people than just its recipients — the true theological beginning, or so I have suggested, of the developed understanding of the sacrifice.

If anyone says that the Mass is useful only to the person who receives communion, and is not to be offered for the living and the dead — for sins, faults, needs for satisfaction, and for any other necessities — let him be anathema.[10]

Father David Power, of the Catholic University of America, has shown that this was, indeed, the central concern of the Fathers of Trent. As he puts it:

The main point of all the definitions is that the Mass celebrated by a duly ordained priest, under whatever circumstances, is beneficial for those for whom it is offered, and that through this offering some grace of remission of sins flows. If this is not admitted, then it was apparently the idea of the Conciliar Fathers that the whole belief in the Mass, and the whole practice of the Mass, would fall apart.[11]

In other words, only if the Mass is a sacrifice can it benefit anyone beyond the immediate partakers, and only if the Mass can benefit people beyond the immediate partakers will the developed eucharistic sensibility and practice of Catholicism make any sense.

After Trent: the questions of theology

In the post-Tridentine period, we can make out four chief concerns corresponding, in part, to the unattended areas of the agenda left by the Master of the Sentences.

1. The sacrifice as ritual

In the first place, people asked: In what ritual respect is the Eucharist a sacrifice? Some theologians, like the Spanish Dominican, Melchior Cano (1520-1560), considered that ritually or liturgically the sacrifice consists of not one but four moments: the consecration of the elements, their subsequent oblation or offering in the Eucharistic Prayer, the fraction of the host and the commingling; and the elements' consumption.[12] If pressed, Cano would lay especial emphasis on the fraction — the breaking, sacramentally, of the Lord's body — for he held that, prior to the fraction, we call the eucharistic action a sacrifice only in the way that we speak of something at hand or close by as if it were present. But, increasingly, theologians rallied to the idea that the ritual moment of the sacrifice is in fact the consecration. More specifically, it is the *separate* consecration of bread and wine — symbolically, of flesh and blood — which signifies the death of the Lord and hence must be

93

the ritual occasion for the making, in sacrament, of his
sacrifice. This is the common doctrine of the great Jesuit
Scholastics so influential after Trent: such men as Alfonso
Salmeron (1515-1585); Gabriel Vasquez (1551-1604); St
Robert Bellarmine (1542-1621), Francis Suarez (1541-1617);
and Leonard Leys or 'Lessius' (1554-1623), who between them
span territory from Andalusia in the south to Flanders in
the north.[13]

2. The sacrifice as reality
Secondly, in what does the Eucharist's sacrificial character
consist — ontologically, and not just liturgically, speaking?
In what way is the rite, at this point, a special epiphany
of being? The Spanish Jesuit, Cardinal John de Lugo (1583-
1660) and his followers claimed that every authentic sacrifice
must involve an act not only of offering but also of
destruction, not only of oblation but of immolation. De Lugo
maintained that, for the Old Testament, whose vocabulary
of sacrificial practice the New Testament makes its own,
all sacrifices manifestly entail such destruction.

The immolation of a living being may recommend itself
as a recognition of God's sovereignty (latreutic sacrifice),
as a propitiation of his offended righteousness (propitiatory
sacrifice) or as a plea for spiritual and temporal blessing
(impetratory sacrifice). The death of Christ was no exception.
De Lugo held that, while Christ, being in glory, can neither
die nor suffer again, he submits nonetheless to a kind of
kenôsis or self-humiliation in consenting to become present
under the sacramental species. By this self-emptying on the
altar he does something analogous to dying and this is what
makes the Eucharist a sacrifice.[14]

A second approach held that the *sacramental* nature of the
ritual immolation suffices to answer our question, achieved
as that sacramental reality is through the separate consecration of bread and wine. Thus two nineteenth century divines,
the Roman theologian Giovanni Perrone (1794–1876), and
John Cuthbert Hedley (1837–1915), monk of Ampleforth and

first bishop of Newport in the restored hierarchy of England
and Wales, considered that the essence of the eucharistic
sacrifice must be sought in the host and the chalice precisely
as consecrated — as affected by an action carried out by
the Church through the ministry of the ordained. As Hedley
wrote:

> The separate consecration, which is the visible work
> of the priest (in the person of Christ) not only pictures
> and represents the blood-shedding of Calvary, but also
> is that (sacramental) 'immutation' of Christ which
> abundantly verifies the conditions of a true sacrifice.

The 'real alteration' of the sacramental conditions of our
Lord's presence — first, through the bread, then through
the wine — makes possible the real sacrifice, that mystical
separation of his body and blood which, as Hedley reminds
us, Gregory Nazianzen had termed *anaimaktos tomê*, a
'bloodless cutting'. The way in which the Church, by the
divine power, brings about the eucharistic conversion *is* the
reality of the eucharistic sacrifice, since that 'way' is a
symbolic slaying of Christ, the true Lamb, in the separate
consecration of bread and wine.[15]

A third group of writers felt the fundamental premise
of the first two lines of thought to be seriously flawed,
for the heart of sacrifice is not destruction but offering.

To find in immolation the pith and marrow of sacrifice
is, they held, offensive to the goodness of the Father. In
the Atonement it is not, strictly speaking, the Son's death
which makes satisfaction for human sins and merits for us
grace and glory, but the loving obedience expressed in the
death. Such writers, and notably the late nineteenth-century
Rhineland theologian Matthias Joseph Scheeben (1835-1888),
held therefore that the only change in the bread and wine
needed to make of them a sacrifice is the bringing to be
of Christ's body and blood on the altar as an act of homage
and honour, directed to the Father. Scheeben, whose theology
is today sadly under-rated,[16] was especially anxious to

emphasise the role, in the eucharistic action, of the Holy Spirit. For the economy of the Son, from Incarnation to Atonement, is dovetailed by that of the Spirit:

> As Christ was conceived of the Holy Spirit, so in the Holy Spirit he offered himself to God undefiled on the Cross, and by the power of the same Holy Spirit he rose again to incorruptible life, in which he eternally displays and guards the value of his sacrificial death.

The Spirit's service of the mission of the Son continues in the eucharistic sacrifice.

> [In order] that this sacrifice [of Calvary], thus brought to pass in the Holy Spirit, may be embodied in the Church and the Church in it, the bread and wine are changed, by the power of the same Holy Spirit and in a renewal and continuation of the mystery of the Incarnation, into the body and blood of the Lamb already immolated and existing as an eternal, perfect holocaust.

And so, Scheeben concludes:

> In this way, Christ, as one who has already gone on ahead by reason of his death and resurrection, is offered to God from the midst of the Church as its sacrifice.[17]

Finally, a school of writers in the Church of France proposed that the essential element in sacrifice is surrender.

Christ had surrendered himself once, in historical time, on Calvary; continually surrenders himself in heaven; and continuously — that is, regularly, very frequently, does so in the Eucharist, as by the hands of his priests he sets forth the same sacrifice in the sacramental separation of his body and blood.[18] Their view was given notably fine expression by the Bavarian theologian Valentin Thalhofer (1825-1891) who wrote of the glorified Christ:

> In his soul, in his will, he retains the wholly willing and obedient renunciatory act of the surrender of his life on earth; and the willing act of his mediation on the Cross abides in him in the form of glory without

strife or bitterness.... That the heavenly sacrifice also relates to the bodily nature of the Lord, that the permanence of the sacrifice of obedience in the soul of Christ must so be manifested somehow in his glorified bodily nature, can be understood of itself. Probably, the marks of the wounds which, according to Scripture and Tradition, Christ still bears in his body on high in heaven, are to be considered as the visible, bodily manifestation of the one abiding sacrifice in the soul.[19]

The act of eucharistic consecration, Thalhofer went on:

has the value and meaning of an act of sacrifice only because of its inner relation to that sacrificial death, which as a willing surrender of life it affirms anew, and continues, and recapitulates.[20]

3. The sacrifice as made in heaven

The conjunction of these texts suggests a third question, also raised by the French school and vital to the evolution of the theology of the eucharistic sacrifice in the age after Trent. What, they asked, is the relation of the Eucharist to the glorified Christ, and not simply to the Christ of Calvary? Such masters of the school as Charles de Condren (1588-1614) and Jean-Jacques Olier (1608-1657) explored this relationship between the eucharistic victim and the transfigured Christ of the eternal sanctuary.[21] Typically, they held that the priestly self-offering of Christ initiated on the Cross was completed or consummated in his exaltation at Easter. They understood the resurrection and ascension as the Father's acceptance of Christ's sacrifice. More especially, the Old Testament practice of burning up ritual victims, so as to mark the consummation of their sacrifice, has as its New Testament counterpart, in their view, that same resurrection and ascension, wherein Christ enters in a definitive way the fire of the Father's love.

The spiritual Jews knew that the victim should be consumed in the most worthy way possible; for besides

97

the command of God to consume it by fire, they knew
that fire was the symbol under which God was hidden;
but only Christians know by faith the true fulfilment
in the glorious resurrection of the body of Jesus Christ,
the consummation of the adorable victim in the truth
which was symbolised by the fire.[22]

Thus the victim present in the Eucharist is the accepted
or exalted victim, the *Christus passus*, or 'Christ who has
suffered', standing in glory before the Father's throne:

This great sacrifice which Jesus Christ in union with
the saints offers to God in heaven, offering himself with
them, is the same sacrifice which the priest offers on
earth, and which the whole Church offers by him in
the holy Mass.[23]

We sometimes find writers of this school attempting to
synthesise their emphasis on the heavenly and eternal self-
offering of Christ in his glory with the notion of sacrifice
as surrender of self, by speaking of Christ's glorification
as the total immolation of his humanity. Olier could write,
therefore, of the exalted Jesus:

Not content with being immolated on Calvary and
giving up his life there, seeing that there still remained
something of the weak nature which he received from
his Mother, he willed to consume it whole on the day
of his Resurrection. Thus it is that he carries religion
to the highest point to which it can go; for he does
not sacrifice a portion of himself only, he offers himself
in a manner so entire and so perfect, that there is nothing
of him left which is not consumed in the glory of his
Father, and annihilated, so to speak, in that devouring
fire of which it is said, 'Our God is a consuming fire'.
Perfect then was the religion of Jesus Christ who
annihilated his whole self in his Father.[24]

Glorification, however, rightly means the *ultimate perfecting*
of the Victim of Calvary, and the apogee of *livingness*. Olier's

words recall, indeed, the argumentation offered by the fourth-century theologian Eusebius of Caesarea to Constantia, sister of the first Christian emperor, Constantine, as to why (in his 'proto-Iconoclast' opinion) Christians may not make an image of the glorified Word Incarnate, for in his risen and ascended existence he has, apparently, put off the finitude of human 'form',[25] or, again, the yet wilder speculations of Eusebius' contemporary, Marcellus of Ancyra, on a final re-integration of the Word into the original unity of the Father — a christological position which Catholics and Orthodox repudiate each Sunday at the Liturgy when, in the Creed, they declare of the Son, 'his kingdom shall have no end'![26] De Condren, accordingly, was careful to say that, if anything is death-like or privative about the condition of Christ in heaven, it is that he was there deprived of mortality and passibility —

> seeing that he then received another life, immortal, impassible, and glorious.[27]

4. The sacrifice as fruitful on earth

The last pervasive question of post-Tridentine theology of the eucharistic sacrifice was, in what sense does the celebrant of the Eucharist have power to apply the fruits of the sacrifice to particular ends within the economies of nature and grace? Can those fruits be explicitly assigned by the Church, acting through the celebrant? In 1786 in the Italian city of Pistoia, a synod, summoned by the civil and religious authorities of Tuscany and under both Gallican and Jansenist influence, declared that whereas, in the Liturgy, specific persons both living and dead may legitimately be prayed for, yet:

> we believe that it is not in the power of the priest to apply the fruits of the sacrifice to whom he wills. Rather we condemn this error as greatly offending against the laws of God who alone distributes the fruits of the sacrifice to those he chooses, and in the measure that pleases him.[27]

Pope Pius VI, however, in his bull of response, *Auctorem fidei*, set aside the view that

> no special fruit of the sacrifice results from that special application which the Church advises and orders to be made on behalf of specific persons, or groups of persons, and particularly by pastors for their flocks.[28]

A major part of the Pope's argumentation turned on appeal to the Church's practice. The Church has acted as if there were such a 'special fruit', and has encouraged the faithful to do the same — for example, by having the Mass offered for 'special intentions'. If no such special fruit existed then the Church's practice would have been grossly defective in a matter touching the central mystery of her existence.

In the course of the nineteenth century, and starting from this lead, it became usual to identify three sorts of 'fruit of the Mass'. First, the *general* or *universal* fruit, for every Mass is offered not only in the person, or name, of the whole Church, but also on behalf of the whole Church. And since all men and women belong potentially to the Church, then indirectly this universal fruit can benefit them all. Secondly, the *special* fruit which pertains to the individual celebrant of the Mass and those of the lay faithful who co-offer with him. Such persons receive blessing as offerers of the sacrifice, and that fruit is no less for one individual just because there are (if this be the case) many people receiving them at the same time. No diminishment reduces the fruit for a worshipper in a crowded basilica, compared with another at a 'house Mass' where two or three are gathered together. Thirdly — and here we meet the element disputed at Pistoia — the Mass can also be offered on specific behalf of definite persons or so as to obtain a given, limited end. For obvious reasons, this came to be called the Mass's 'intermediate fruit', since it is neither, on the one hand, universal, nor, on the other, narrowly limited to the actual offerers at the particular Mass. This fruit depends on the free disposition, or application, of the celebrant. Most theologians accepted that the intermediate fruit is lessened for individuals if the Mass be applied on behalf of many persons at the same time. Once again, the grounds for this conviction were the Church's practice. By custom, the Mass is usually offered for one, or for a few, persons. Yet were the intermediate fruit unlimited in extent, such a custom would be hurtful to souls. Without any reason, some people would be excluded from participation in the more particular benefit which the Mass could bring.[29] It is, of course, this notion of the intermediate fruit of the sacrifice which underlies the current, and by no means wholly satisfactory, practice of giving and receiving Mass-stipends. Although a reform of the stipendiary system is long overdue, it could be carried out, in the opinion of this writer, without damage to a teaching which forms part of the ordinary magisterial doctrine of the Church, and has strong backing from the sense of the faithful wherever a feeling for the Mass as sacrifice remains lively.[30] Thus, for instance, it could reasonably be required that where a stipend is transferred to another celebrant, the concrete intention for which the offering was given must remain attached. The question of the intermediate fruit, under other names, will crop up again, as we shall see, in the eucharistic theology of the twentieth century.

6

Catholic Eucharistic Theology in the Twentieth Century

1. Theological *ressourcement*

At one level, the achievement of twentieth-century eucharistic theology is simply the retrieval of what was best in the eucharistic doctrine of the preceding nineteen centuries. The themes of eucharistic theology were already well established before the twentieth century opened. As we have followed them, they are: the Eucharist as foundation of the Church; the real presence and its rationale or purposes; and the real sacrifice and its benefits. But these themes were not equally well handled by all earlier theologians. Twentieth-century writers, therefore, set themselves to recover the best features of their predecessors and to inter-relate them in a way that was intellectually coherent, theologically balanced, and preachable — understandable by the committed Catholic Christian, of average intelligence, willing to take trouble to find out about the faith. In this sense, a classic example of the best twentieth-century eucharistic theology might be the little book, *A Key to the Doctrine of the Eucharist* by the Benedictine Anscar Vonier, Abbot of Buckfast, which first saw the light of day in 1925.[1]

The most important gain of such *ressourcement*, 'returning to the sources', in eucharistic theology was the sane and splendid account of the inter-relation of the Supper, the Cross and the Church's sacrifice offered by the French Jesuit Maurice de la Taille, and, in dependence on his work, in an attractive native version by the Anglo-Welsh writer and artist David Jones. For De la Taille, it was in the Supper that Christ ritually offered the sacrifice of his Passion.[2] 'Victimhood' includes both an act of offering, and an immolation: the total act of sacrifice must embrace both. But this raises the question:

> Where or when did Christ perform that voluntary and active dedication of himself to the worship of God as Victim, sensibly, liturgically and ritually... By what external act did Christ assume the bearing of a priest towards his Passion; by what rite did he offer the sacrifice?[3]

Recounting how various earlier divines, from Ephraem Syrus to the age of Aquinas have had a stab at answering this question (Christ's causing the soldiers in the garden to fall prostrate, as described in John 18:6, or the death-cry 'in a loud voice', of Mark 15:37), De la Taille shows that the overwhelming testimony of Scripture, the Fathers and the Church's approved theologians locates that act of offering elsewhere: in the drama of the Supper.[4] In imagistic action, Christ offered himself for his coming immolation, and was in that moment given over, in fullest reality, into the ownership of God, dedicated to the Passion, deputed to an expiatory death for the salvation of humankind. And drawing on the liturgies of East and West, De la Taille concludes:

> He offered himself to be immolated, in order that we may offer him immolated, and that we may be nourished with the flesh and blood of the Immolated.[5]

In other words, not only is the undivided action of the Redemption to be found in the Supper and the Passion *together* (because, in the Supper, Christ offered his own body to the death in blood he was to undergo on the Cross); the Supper, as the offering of him who was to be immolated, *oblatio victimae immolandae*, is the prefiguration and promise of the Eucharist, the offering of the now immolated Victim, *oblatio victimae immolatae*, in sacramental form.

For De la Taille, the claim of the Council of Trent that, as between Calvary and the eucharistic sacrifice, the victim is the same, only the manner of offering different, has its ultimate ground in the relation between the Last Supper and the Cross. There were not two offerings: the same offering was made ritually in the Supper, and continued morally on the Cross where Christ sealed and confirmed, robed and crowned it. And this is thanks to the identity of the Priest and the Victim:

> a rational Victim whose constant will in suffering unto death was none other than the continued will of the Priest, faithful in sacrifice to the end.[6]

The Supper differs, via the Cross, from the Mass in two aspects only: firstly, there Christ offered without us, whereas in the Eucharist he offers through us; and, secondly, because while the Supper looked to the immolation as future, the Mass looks to it as past.

David Jones, a tertiary of the Dominican order, discovered the work of De la Taille in the course of his own investigations of man as a maker and user of signs — vital to him not only as a eucharistic worshipper but as poet and artist as well. Like the author of *Mysterium fidei*, Jones linked the pragmatic action of Christ's bloody self-surrender on the Cross to the artistic devising of the sacrament in the Upper Room, and both to the Eucharist of the Church. Referring to the sporadic recurrence, in non-Catholic Christianity, of anti-sacramental convictions, Jones remarked:

> It has been and is argued by many that the actual lifting up of the *Signum* on the Hill put an end to all need of further *signs*. This sounds convincing until we consider what was done at the Supper, when it seems no longer tenable. For in the Cenacle the Victim himself did something and said something which no matter how it is theologically interpreted and no matter what its inter-relatedness to what was done on the Hill, was unmistakably and undeniably a sign-making and a rite-making, and so an act of Ars; moreover an act to be, in some sense, repeated.[7]

Not only as human beings, then, but, more particularly, as Christians are we committed to the notion of sign. And, more specifically still, for Jones, as *Catholic* Christians we hold that the Redeemer, on the day before he suffered, involved the redeemed in 'an act of *Ars*', and involved them so intimately that the benefits of 'what was done on the Hill' are chiefly mediated through a continuation of the sign-making of the Upper Room.

Using his own favoured terms of 'utile' (pragmatic) and 'extra-utile' (symbolic), David Jones not only joined these three 'moments' — Last Supper, Calvary, Eucharist — in the coming to be of the sacramental sacrifice. Albeit with the necessary distinctions, he *identified* them. Looking back on his work in 1971, near the end of his life, he wrote to his friend Harman Grisewood of:

> this pivot round which all one has ever stated depends, this utterly crucial matter, the distinction between the utile and the extra-utile, between, at its highest conceivable level ... the *oblatio* at the Supper, a ritual act and wholly extra-utile, and the entirely utile acts whereby he who was already self-oblated was made fast by iron hooks to the wood of the *stauros* [the Cross]. We speak of the 'Altar of the Cross' only on the *presupposition* that the extra-utile ritual oblation at the Supper had already placed our Lord in the state of a victim awaiting immolation.

Unless the in-utile and the utile are co-involved in the work of our redemption

> the rite at the Supper and the execution on the Tree have no substantial connection nor, necessarily, the Sacrifice of the Mass with both. Whereas we [Catholics] are committed to something more than a connection of some sort, but rather to an actual, real (substantive) identity under differing forms.[8]

Jones' distinctive contribution, made most fully in his poetry,

105

was to suggest the wider — the widest possible — context for De la Taille's theological *ressourcement*. What was accomplished on Calvary 'presupposes the sign-world' looking back to millennia of foreshadowing rites and arts, just as the whole world that Christ was redeeming involved all humanity, 'from before Swanscombe Man to after Atomic Man' in that act.[9]

It would not, however, be right to leave the topic of *ressourcement* in eucharistic theology without adverting to the remarkable revival, in twentieth-century Catholicism — as also Eastern Orthodoxy — of eucharistic ecclesiology.

Although the post-mediaeval Western tradition was not unaware of the Eucharist-Church connection, it became a somewhat marginalised motif until the rise of the 'liturgical movement' of the early twentieth century. Writing on the eve of the Great War, one observer lamented:

> Contemporary authors seem not to have attached much importance to this unitive power of the Eucharist. If *L'Année Liturgique* and a few occasional mystical writings had not taken care to relaunch it into circulation, it would have become, in our time, a forgotten doctrine.[10]

Harvesting the riches of the patristic and mediaeval tradition in both West and East, Vatican II, that great monument to *ressourcement*, wrote a eucharistic ecclesiology into its own documents. Three texts from *Lumen Gentium,* its Dogmatic Constitution on the Church, may suffice as witnesses to its presence there. The fathers of the Second *Vaticanum* affirm:

> As often as the sacrifice of the Cross by which 'Christ our Pasch is sacrificed' is celebrated on the altar, the work of our redemption is carried out. Likewise, in the sacrament of the eucharistic Bread, the unity of believers, who form one body in Christ, is both expressed and brought about.
>
> Really sharing in the body of the Lord in the breaking of the eucharistic Bread, we are taken up into communion with him and with one another.

Then, strengthened by the body of Christ in the eucharistic communion, they manifest in a concrete way that unity of the People of God which this holy sacrament aptly signifies and admirably realises.[11]

In the contemporary period, Catholic and Orthodox theology have achieved a remarkable convergence, through privileging the relation of the Eucharist to the Church as a key to ecclesiology. On the Orthodox side, one has the example of such recent or living authors as Nikolai Afanas'ev, George Florovsky, Paul Evdokimov and John Meyendorff (all theologians of the Russian Diaspora), as well as a Greek theologian, originally writing as a layman but now a bishop of the Holy Synod of the Ecumenical Patriarchate, John Zizioulas. On the Catholic side outstanding names would include the Jesuit cardinal Henri de Lubac, the Oratorian Louis Bouyer, the Dominican Yves Congar, and the Benedictine Emmanuel Lanne, monk of Chevetogne (the bi-ritual 'Monastery of Reunion', dedicated to the overcoming of the Latin-Byzantine schism), as well as the Bavarian theologian, now Prefect of the (Roman) Congregation for the Doctrine of the Faith, Joseph Ratzinger.[12] It was scarcely a coincidence, therefore, that the first meeting of the Orthodox-Catholic ecumenical commission, established in 1980, should have taken as its theme, 'The Mystery of the Church and the Eucharist in the Light of the Mystery of the Holy Trinity'.[13]

2. New issues
At another level, when we speak of twentieth-century eucharistic theology, we have in mind theology which is peculiar to the twentieth century: theological issues concerning the Eucharist which have not been raised before or, at any rate, not in their modern form.

Three such issues have been much discussed:

(a) The one Mass and the many celebrations
This is the problem, raised by the late Karl Rahner, of how

we may justify the private celebration of Mass once we have accepted the insights of the Liturgical Movement into how the Mass is essentially a community affair.[14] This question of the standing of the private celebration may seem purely a matter of liturgical spirituality — something personally trying for older or more conservative priests, but in fact it has wider ramifications. These further dimensions are partly practical: if a priest cannot celebrate, or con-celebrate, a congregational Mass each day, should he refrain from celebrating altogether? Trying to answer this question takes us beyond the prosaic issue of a priest's horary to realms theological. What are the implications of a liturgically-based refusal to celebrate privately for the traditional notion that every Mass, whether of a bishop with the local Church in full assembly, or of a hermit without so much as a server, is a sacramental sacrifice which benefits the living and the dead?

To say that the Eucharist is a real sacrifice is to affirm that in the Mass the unique sacrifice of the Son on Good Friday, accepted by the Father at Easter, becomes present, and not just present, but efficaciously so. Through this sacramental sacrifice, the fruits of Christ's self-offering are given anew to the whole Church, and in a special way to the participants, and to those for whom the Mass is offered, those, as the Roman Canon puts it 'for whom we offer, or who themselves offer unto you this sacrifice of praise'. Though it may be spiritually uncongenial for a priest to celebrate by himself (normally, with a server), it is, seemingly, always spiritually beneficial for the Church that he should do so. When in 1949 Karl Rahner queried that this conclusion really followed, he came for the first time to the unfavourable attention of Pope Pius XII and the Roman curia.[15] Rahner pointed out that for the Mass to be a genuine sacrifice, enacted in the power of Jesus Christ and his Spirit, does not mean that it applies the fruits of Calvary in some automatic fashion. Like all grace, the grace of this sacrifice requires human co-operation, and in this particular case such co-operation will take the form of devotion or (in more contemporary idiom) receptivity. Only through the devotion of those sharing in the sacrifice, whether as celebrant (or con-celebrant), lay co-offerer or provider of the stipend, does the Mass yield up the blessings of the Atonement. If a particular form of the Mass-ritual ceases to arouse devotion — since through improved liturgical understanding priests and people come to see its deficiencies — then there is no reason to think that such a Mass does in fact bestow the grace of Christ's death and Resurrection on those for whom it is offered.

Rahner was right in his assertion that the liturgical fullness of the Eucharist is found only in a Mass with a congregation — above all in the bishop's Mass, with presbyters, deacons, possibly lay ministers and certainly the whole local people taking their proper part. Vatican II, in its Dogmatic Constitution on the Liturgy, would later give solemn sanction to the principal aim of the Liturgical Movement, namely, the restoration of the ideal of corporate worship: the people of God in a local place assembled in their hierarchical order as the body of Christ. And yet, as such critics of Rahner as the Irish Dominican Colman O'Neill were not slow to point out, the practical provisions of the liturgical reform, however harmonious with the logic of the sacramental system, and with human nature at large, can only have a relative value.[16] They are instruments, there to help the Christian enter more fully into the mystery of the Mass as foundation of the Church, as presence, and as sacrifice. Moreover, since the Mass is a mystery it transcends not only every form of linguistic description we may venture but also every form of ritual participation whereby we celebrate it. O'Neill accepted that there can be no Eucharist without the Christian community, but he denied that the community could only be present in an empirical, congregational form. The whole Church offers every Eucharist, even a privately celebrated one, and the whole Church draws benefit from the offering.

But so far the last statements are sheerest as assertion. *How* does the whole Church offer and benefit from every Mass? O'Neill agreed with Rahner that the eucharistic application of the fruits of Calvary depends on the receptivity of the Church's members — a receptivity itself the result of God's grace. As he expressed it, the faithful have

> a determinative role in the assessment of any Mass's effective value. The infinite value of Calvary is applied to the Church and the world in proportion to the devotion of the faithful expressed in the Church's sacrifice.[17]

To O'Neill's mind, Rahner's mistake lay in the restrictiveness whereby he confined this 'devotion of the faithful' to those faithful alone who were linked directly to a particular celebration — either by taking part in it directly, or, as stipend-givers by providing the *oblatio*, the material means whereby the celebration can take place.

O'Neill pointed out that neither Pius XII's letter *Mediator Dei* of 1947, on the Liturgy, nor Paul VI's *Mysterium fidei* of 1965, on the Holy Eucharist, was easily reconciled here with Rahner's teaching. For Pius XII implicitly, for Paul VI explicitly, each Mass is the offering of the entire Church. O'Neill's account of how this may be so is couched in terms of the representative character of the celebrant. As *Mediator Dei* puts it,

> The celebrant in offering acts in the name both of Christ and of the faithful, of whom the divine Redeemer is the head.[18]

Now, as we know, the faithful who share liturgically in a given Eucharist offer with the ordained minister. Though the non-ordained depend on the ordained for the making present of Christ's sacrifice, once that glorious offering is made present they co-offer it in virtue of the royal and universal priesthood of the baptised which is theirs. But — and this is the point O'Neill desired to press home — other faithful who do not share liturgically in a given Mass may still be said to offer it through, though not with, the celebrant. By the sacrament of Order there is a real if mysterious link joining the celebrant to all the members of the Church, involving the latter in every celebration according to the measure of their receptivity: a coinherence of the one and the many in the mystical heart of the sacramental economy. Paradoxically, Rahner's view, in seeking to defend the corporate nature of the Eucharist, fails to appreciate the true depths of the corpus, the social body of the Church. Or, as O'Neill puts it, more combatively, the very individualism and subjectivism now rejected as opposed to the authentic sense of the Liturgy now revive among those who sincerely believe themselves to be the foremost proponents of the liturgical spirit.

(b) Fresh theories of the eucharistic presence
The second novel element in twentieth-century eucharistic theology concerns not so much the sacrifice as the presence, and not so much the rationale of the presence but its mode. And this is the attempt to find an alternative philosophical language in which to express something of the Church's faith about the 'marvellous change' called by Lateran Four and Trent 'transubstantiation'. The two main contenders for the post of possible supplanter of the language of transubstantiation were 'trans-signification' and 'trans-finalisation'. As their names suggest, they mean, respectively, 'the changing of a sign' and 'the changing of a purpose'. Put forward in rather obscure Dutch catechetical and devotional reviews in the 1950s, these notions are most easily accessible in the second part of Father Edward Schillebeeckx's *The Eucharist*.[20]

Transfinalisation takes its rise from a piece of biblical theology. Insofar as the Bible has its own metaphysic, so writers of this kind maintain, it is a metaphysic of divine purpose. For these authors, who depend in some degree on the seminal study, *Ceci est mon corps*, by the distinguished

111

Calvinist systematician and ecumenist Franz Leenhardt,[21] the substance of any reality always lies in the divine intention realised within it. What something is must ultimately be identified in terms of the divine purpose it serves. Ordinary bread serves God's purpose of sustaining members of the human race through the material resources of his creation. Therefore, ordinary bread *is* such material sustenance. Eucharistic bread, by contrast, serves God's purpose of feeding man spiritually with the life of his Son. Therefore, eucharistic bread *is* the life of the Son as communicated to human beings. The words of consecration, on this theory, are God's declaration of his change of purpose in regard to the elements. The eucharistic conversion is really trans-finalisation, a change of purpose.

Two drawbacks of this idea may be mentioned. In the first place, by stressing so strongly the sovereignty of God over the creatures he has made, transfinalisation is ever in peril of collapsing into a kind of reverent agnosticism. It carries back an English mind to the adage ascribed to Elizabeth I: 'What his word doth make it, that I believe and take it'. That rhyme, whoever composed it, captures the spirit of the Elizabethan settlement in religion: a refusal to choose between competing doctrines, except by excluding the two 'extremes' of Anabaptism and Roman Catholicism. Secondly, trans-finalisation language blurs the distinction between, in more classical theological terms, a 'dynamist' or 'virtualist' and a truly 'realist' account of the presence of Jesus Christ in the consecrated elements. If what is present in the Eucharist is simply the saving power or action of the Saviour, then the Eucharist is on all fours with the other sacraments. We deprive it of its unique status as the only sacramental gift which actually contains the Giver.[22] If, however, these drawbacks are duly registered and allowed for, the more traditional ontological concepts may be invoked to supplement the deficiencies of the newer notion.

Trans-signification, the more discussed of the two twentieth century theories, appears to have taken its rise from an unpublished study by Père Yves de Montcheuil, SJ, entitled 'La présence réelle' and circulated in manuscript form after its author's execution as a member of the French Resistance movement in 1944.[23] Unlike trans-finalisation, it owes its conceptual starting-point not to biblical theology but to contemporary philosophy and, more especially, to phenomenology. Phenomenology is an account of being as meaning. It does not attempt to describe the intrinsic structure of reality, the nature of things, but rather to evoke the significance of being for a human participator. One major interest of phenomenologists has been the many-faceted phenomenon of the symbol, and, correspondingly, a favoured phenomenological view of the human being has been the symbol-making animal. By fashioning symbols, we express ourselves, and in this way our interiority, our inner attitude, comes to be for us for (it may be) the first time. Furthermore, through such symbols - which might range from a handshake to a Botticelli — human beings enter into communication with each other. Through the medium of the symbol, their reality comes to be in a reciprocally recognised manner.

Thus the Dutch Capuchin Father Luchesius Smits has proposed that Christ as man symbolically expressed his love for his disciples in the bread and wine of the Supper, such that the bread and wine became the medium of a meeting between his friends and himself at a new level of human depth.[24] Those media, however, as signs of Christ's human love, are not yet what the Church means by 'the holy Gifts'. For Christ is not only man; he is the Son of God. Consequently, the consecrated bread and wine signify the love of the God-man for us. Thus the encounter they mediate is a unique meeting with One who is God, and the means of such a meeting enjoy, therefore, a unique status, incomparably more exalted than any other social meal — and more privileged, indeed, than any other symbol. Smits emphasised, in a way reminiscent of the Paschasian tradition in early mediaeval eucharistic theology, that Incarnation and Eucharist form one single, self-identical mystery. In becoming man, the Son incarnated the saving design of the Father, and he continues this incarnation by choosing certain things — bread, wine — as extensions of his humanity.

Supporters of trans-signification are understandably at pains to distinguish their teaching from that of earlier symbolists to whom Paschasian incarnationalism could be but uncomfortably yoked, such as Berengar. Such earlier symbolists had properly incurred the Church's condemnation, lacking the advantage as they did of a phenomenological understanding of signs. An attenuated notion of symbol thinks of a sign as merely a signal, something pointing to a reality outside and other than itself, the red light on a railway signals pointing to a train travelling in the opposite direction. The Church was right to lay aside that account, and to insist on something more. Unfortunately, so trans-significationists allege, Christian Scholasticism misinterpreted this legitimate demand for 'something more'. Scholastic theologians imagined that the only alternative to a symbol-presence of Christ in the Eucharist was the form of presence characteristic not of persons but of things. And so it was that trans-substantiation arose, the substance or 'thinginess' of bread and wine declared displaced by the substance of Christ himself.

What are we to make of trans-signification and its attempt to replace trans-substantiation as the central Catholic accounts of the eucharistic presence? First, a word about this from the standpoint of 'fundamental' theology, and, more particularly, on the role of philosophical theories in the expression of doctrine. It may be said at once that the Church's teaching office has no authority to impose a philsophical system, such as Aristotelian Thomism (essentially, a Platonised Aristotelianism modified by the introduction of the notion of creation) on all Catholic divines. Certainly, there are a number of truths normally called philosophical like, say, the immortality of the soul, which revelation presupposes and which can therefore appropriately be taught by the Church. But this liberty of the magisterium does not extend so far as to embrace an entire philosophical system, or even the particular way in which a truth assumed by revelation is incorporated into such a given system. We must distinguish, then, between, on the one hand, the systematic philosophical exposition of a natural truth vital to revelation, and that natural truth itself — apprehended, we might say, spontaneously or pre-philosophically by human beings in various cultures or situations. In the example offered above, that of the soul's deathlessness, the Fifth Lateran Council teaches that the immortality of the soul can be known with certainty by natural reason, yet refrains from specifying by what kind of philosophy such an apprehension or judgement should be expounded. Returning, then, to the matter of the Eucharist: granted that the Church should not oblige her theologians to do theology using the technical Aristotelian-Thomist concepts of substance and accidents, is she obliged, nevertheless, to defend what can by called the *non-technical content* of those concepts, so as to safeguard her faith in the eucharistic presence, with all that means for her life and mission?

It is not a piece of specialised philosophy but a matter of common-sense judgement that things exist independently of the thinking subject. Revelation confirms this common sense judgment by the doctrine of creation which tells me that the ground of the independence I ascribe to the things I know is the triune God. If I say that a thing manifests itself to me as enjoying independent existence as the particular kind of being it is, I implicitly affirm that it is a substance. What issues from the creative act in enjoyment of a particular form of independent existence is a substance. In the case of the Eucharist, the Church safeguards her confession of faith in the presence by insisting, *inter alia*, that the independent reality of things be duly recognised. Without such recognition, we cannot speak of the eucharistic change as taking place where it most profoundly does: at the level of the creative activity of God touching this bread and this wine.[25]

115

This does not, however, render the theologies of trans-signification and trans-finalisation otiose, much less rule them wholly out of court. A phenomenological account of how the Father's saving design becomes incarnate in the symbol-making activity purposed by the Son is not wrong-headed or ecclesially undesirable. It is, however, by itself inadequate and needs supplementation if it is to do justice to the faith of the Church. This was Paul VI's conviction in the writing of *Mysterium fidei:*

> When transubstantiation has taken place, the appearances of bread and wine acquire, beyond doubt, a new meaning and a new finality. They are no longer ordinary bread and ordinary drink, but the symbol of a created thing and the symbol of spiritual nourishment. But if they acquire a new significance and a new finality, it is because they contain a new reality which we justly call 'ontological'.[26]

The importance of this adjudication can be tested by asking two questions. First, how does the Eucharist bring about the actual presence of Christ to his Church? A gift, which is how trans-significationists, with some justification from tradition, see the eucharistic elements, presupposes, either here or elsewhere in the world of experience, the bodily presence of the giver. Although the Eucharist cannot bring us bodily contact with Christ in his natural reality, it none the less approaches such contact by transcending the order of sheer giving activity. It is, precisely, *presence.* Within the being of the Holy Gifts there is, in sacramental form, the person of the giver himself, and to express this we must go beyond a phenomenological analysis of gift-giving. Secondly, where does the eucharistic sacrifice appear in this approach? As an account of holy communion trans-signification makes much sense: Christ mediates himself in the gift wherein we encounter him. But in the Eucharist Christ is not simply offered to us; he is also offered to the Father. The Eucharist can only be for the Church what

Christ's death was for the Son of God if the Lord is truly present as victim on the altar. In this way, the doctrine of the real sacrifice is a touchstone for the adequacy of a theology of the real presence. No story of the presence which fails to display the sacrifice will do. In eucharistic communion, Christ offers us his friendship to unite us together. But this friendship is that of the head of the mystical body associating his members with his own sacrifice. And this demands a new form of being-in-the-world for the risen Christ. He gives himself a new bodily presence among us in the form of a victim, entering the reality of our world, transubstantiating into his own personal life our human food, in bread and wine.[27]

(c) The Eucharist and social justice
Thirdly, and the most recent arrival among the new themes, is the relation between the Eucharist and human solidarity: notably, in the perspective of 'liberation theology', of the claims of justice. The founder of that controverted movement, the Peruvian Gustavo Gutiérrez, considered the Eucharist somewhat briefly in the study which gave liberation theology its name. On our subject, Gutiérrez finds four pillars for his wisdom: the background to the Last Supper in the Jewish Passover, with its commemoration of the exodus from Egypt; the Johannine narrative of the foot-washing, seen as the 'profound meaning of the eucharistic celebration'; the significant coincidence whereby *koinônia*, Paul's term for eucharistic participation is also his word for the collection for the poor of the Jerusalem Church, and our Lord's command, recorded by St Matthew, to reconcile oneself with one's brother prior to laying one's gift upon the altar. Building on these foundations, Gutiérrez declares the 'celebration of the Lord's Supper and the creation of human brotherhood' to be 'inseparably joined'.[28]

In the earlier editions of *Teología de la Liberación*, Gutiérrez seemed to give the stamp of his theological approval to a claim by the French Marxist philosopher Louis Althusser

117

(d.1990) that the notion of the Church's unity functions as a 'myth' which must disappear if the Church is to be 're-converted' to the service of the workers in the class struggle.[29] The conclusion drawn by some that the *res* of the Eucharist as charity is beyond reach in a context of social or social-ideological division at the Synaxis, the eucharistic assembly, was rightly challenged by the Congregation for the Doctrine of the Faith in its *Instruction on Certain Aspects of the 'Theology of Liberation'*.[30]

It remains true, none the less, that eucharistic participation has its ethical preconditions and entailments, as the Eucharist's intimate connection with the sacrament of Penance bears witness. And such preconditions and entailments are not least a matter of the virtues relevant to the social reign of Christ.

> Would you honour the body of Christ? Do not despise his nakedness; do not honour him here in church clothed in silk vestments and then pass him by unclothed and frozen outside... What is the use of loading Christ's table with gold cups while he himself is starving? Feed the hungry and then if you have any money left over, spend it on the altar table.[31]

If, where acceptable, Gutiérrez's claims for a relation between the Eucharist and social justice seem rather general, these words of St John Chryostom may serve as a bridge to another writer concerned with this theme. Father Edward Kilmartin, SJ, an American historian of the primitive liturgy, has seized on the feature of the *collection* (still called, in Italian, for instance, 'the alms') to give a liberation-theological understanding of the Eucharist greater specificity. As he writes:

> Inserted into the memorial of the sacrifice of Christ, the offering of gifts should be an expression of thanksgiving to God, a consecration of the material world and human work to God. At the same time, it becomes an expression of the truth that true service of God always involves the service of humankind.[32]

Through the gifts, the donor expresses 'his or her priestly service of God and God's poor'. Accordingly, the ministerial priest who receives the collection at the altar should distribute it likewise to the poor — though in this formulation, the wider destinies of the collection, as Kilmartin has described them earlier, seem lost to view. Suggesting that the pooling of monies for other ends, such as church building or education, might more appropriately be done in some other context, he asks that the community take it for granted that 'the normal recipients are God's poor', thus broadening the horizon of its social obligations beyond the needs of its own members or those of its clergy.

If the Roman offertory procession stimulated these thoughts in the American liturgist, his fellow-countryman, F.X. Meehan, of St Charles' Seminary, Philadelphia, presents a rather fuller theology of the Eucharist — albeit in a highly impressionistic idiom — in the context of a 'social spirituality'. Seeing the Eucharist as irreplaceable source of the gift of unity in a 'work where unity is always threatened', Meehan pleads for a recovery of a lively sense of the Eucharist as *sacrifice*, since 'the work for the poor takes place in a desert and in a dark night'. The Spirit who gives unity comes from the pierced side of the crucified Lord and his Supper — sometimes, in recent years, too trivially enacted in the cheap grace of an over-facile celebration of community — is a sacrificial meal given to us on the day before he suffered. In the Eucharist, Christ is present not so much 'in glory, but as a pledge of glory'.[33] And so in this last writer of the liberation theological school to be cited here we are returned — but with a genuine increase of understanding — to the profound theology of the eucharistic sacrifice with which twentieth-century reflection on this mystery opened.

7

A Systematic Summary: Balthasar and John Paul II

O Trinity! Eternal Trinity! Fire, abyss of love!
Would it not have been enough to create us
after your own image and likeness,
making us reborn through grace
by the blood of your Son?

Was it necessary that you should give
even the Holy Trinity as food for souls?

Yet, your love willed this, O eternal Trinity.
You gave us not only your Word
through the Redemption and in the Eucharist.
But you also gave yourself
In your fullness of love for your creature.[1]

These words of St Catherine of Siena remind us that, for the instinct of faith, the Eucharist belongs — not in spite, but because of its own specific themes — to the totality of the economy of salvation and, thereby, to the disclosure of the divine glory which is salvation's end.[2]

Of contemporary doctors it is, above all, the Swiss theologian Hans Urs von Balthasar who has most effectively re-placed the eucharistic themes — presence, sacrifice, foundation of the Church — in this wider context which the rapturous hymnody and prayer of Catherine open to us. As one of Balthasar's foremost English exponents, John Saward, has written, by way of exposition of this master's thought:

The Eucharist has its presupposition in the Trinity. In the inner life of the Godhead, the divine essence which

the Son eternally receives from the Father he offers
back to him in gratitude, in love, in the Holy Spirit.
The Son is thanksgiving in his very person, 'the Father's
substantial Eucharist'.[3]

For Balthasar, if the very being of the pre-existent Son can
be called 'eucharistic', since the Son is from all eternity
the *thankful* Son, who responds 'eucharistically' to his own
generation as the Word of God, then this condition of his
is both reflected and extended by Christ's earthly action
in that Word's incarnate life. Jesus lives eucharistically as
man: he presents himself as the self-giving one, and this,
his most characteristic trait, comes to its consummation in
his Passion.

During the Passion's prelude and initiation, the Supper,
Christ offers his body to be broken, his blood to be poured
out. This essentially eucharistic character of the Son's divine
and human existence is, moreover, altogether relevant to
ourselves, for:

> In offering his body for us, in giving his body to us,
> the thankful Son fulfils his Father's will that we be
> drawn into the life of the Blessed Trinity.[4]

In the sacramental medium of the Eucharist, he continues
to offer his life for us, glorified though his manhood now
is, with the same gesture of sacrificial love which he made
once for all on the Cross. As Balthasar writes

> He was once given, slain on the Cross, poured out,
> pierced, will never take back his gift, his gift of himself.
> He will never gather into himself his eucharistic
> fragmentation in order to be one with himself. Even
> as the risen Lord he lives as the One who has given
> himself and has poured himself out.[5]

Only if the Eucharist comprises at once true sacrifice and
real presence can it be, in other words, the trinitarian and
christological foundation of the Church.

To move from the Swiss dogmatician to the Polish pope
is no arduous journey. The pontiff who set himself to re-
create the Catholic pattern from the sometimes bewildering
kaleidoscope of the immediately post-Conciliar Church has
made no secret of his admiration for Balthasar's work. Not
only did he award him the first papal prize in theology
— itself named for a pope whose eucharistic teaching we
have had occasion to cite more than once, Paul VI. He also
pressed him to receive the cardinalate, though the
octogenarian priest-theologian died, suddenly enough, a few
days before that honour could be conferred. (The Pope
insisted that, none the less, he be buried as a cardinal-presbyter
of the Roman Church, and so he lies, in the family grave
at Lucerne.) The themes of foundation, sacrifice, presence,
for which Balthasar sought to disclose the gracious
underpinning in the life and action of the triune God, and
of the Saviour, are orchestrated in more subdued tonality
by the Pope in his letter, *Eucharisticum mysterium*, 'On the
Mystery and Worship of the Holy Eucharist'. The text can
count as a miniature compendium of the doctrinal
development whose story we have traced in this book, for
it revolves around the Eucharist's three great themes as here
identified.[6]

Taking them in the order of foundation, sacrifice, presence,
the Pope begins his dogmatic exposition with the apparent
paradox that while the Church 'makes the Eucharist', it
is the Eucharist which 'builds up the Church'. From Holy
Thursday until the dawning of the Last Day, the Church's
pilgrimage is made possible by the Holy Eucharist.

> The Church was founded, as the new community of
> the People of God, in the apostolic community of those
> Twelve who, at the Last Supper, became partakers of
> the Body and Blood of the Lord under the species of
> bread and wine. Christ had said to them, 'Take and
> eat ... take and drink'. And carrying out this command
> of his, they entered for the first time into sacramental
> communion with the Son of God, a communion that

is a pledge of eternal life. From that moment until the end of time, the Church is being built up through that same communion with the Son of God, a communion which is a pledge of the eternal Passover.[7]

Guarding against a possible reductionist misunderstanding of this claim, the Pope insists that, while the experience of eucharistic brotherhood indeed belongs to this foundation, it is not its deepest reality. For the human *koinônia* of the eucharistic assembly is not its own ground. We must look further, and here the Pope comes to the other two principal themes of eucharistic doctrine, the sacrifice and the presence. As he writes:

> The Church is brought into being when, in that fraternal union and communion, we celebrate the Sacrifice of the Cross of Christ, when we proclaim 'the Lord's death until he comes', and later, when, being deeply compenetrated with the mystery of our salvation, we approach as a community the table of the Lord, in order to be nourished there, in a sacramental manner, by the fruits of the Holy Sacrifice of propitiation.[8]

Because the mystery of the Eucharist, as foundation, sacrifice and presence, is centred on the Cross, the Tree of Life, the ethos of eucharistic worship is evangelical to its very core. The Eucharist, so the Pope concludes, educates in love, and, for those who receive it worthily — that is, with repentance and joy — it creates true witnesses of Christ.

> Eucharistic worship is not so much worship of the inaccessible transcendence as worship of the divine condescension, and it is also the merciful and redeeming transformation of the world in the human heart.[9]

It is for this that we celebrate the Eucharist with all reverence — just as it is for this that, in our study, we have followed the course of the doctrine of the Holy Eucharist, from its origin in the life of the Founder of Christianity, to its estuary in the practice and understanding of the present-day Church.

May there be further, future, development in the understanding of what the Roman liturgy calls *hoc magnum mysterium*, 'this great mystery'? We can hope that the Spirit, who leads the Church into all the truth, will facilitate ampler and more lucid insight into this 'everlasting covenant'. But we know that what lies ahead must be, in the authentic tradition of the Church, consonant with what has gone before. Tradition is life-giving memory, and for it nothing once known can be forgotten, nothing once accepted rejected. The Woman as old as the ages is wise in the telling of her story, and, with its resources can be, in every new generation, the ever-youthful Bride.

Appendix

The Eucharist in Anglicanism

At no period in the history of the Church of England, matrix of the Anglican Communion, has there been real consensus about the meaning of what is done in the Eucharist. The underlying reason for this is the pluriform nature of the English Reformation, which comprised elements deriving from late mediaeval dissent (the Lollards), elements stemming from Continental influence (first Lutheran, then Calvinist), and elements that took their source from the idea of a national Catholicism — all held together by the Crown, which claimed the same rights to order the Church as those maintained by the Roman and Byzantine emperors since Constantine.

The Eucharist of the Book of Common Prayer (the Second Prayer Book of Edward VI, 1552), a rite composed in all essentials by the first Protestant archbishop of Canterbury, Thomas Cranmer, was intended by its author to be taken in a Zwinglian sense.[1] Cranmer desired no eucharistic sacrifice; and accepted no real presence — not even the 'virtual presence', or presence of Christ's power, favoured by Calvinists. However, Article 28 of the Elizabethan 39 Articles, produced after Cranmer's execution by Mary Tudor, implicitly rejects Zwinglianism, thus ensuring that the Anglican Church began life with an internally inconsistent view of the Eucharist.[2] As in so much, it was Richard Hooker who attempted to carve out a distinctive Anglican *via media* — as between, by the later years of Elizabeth's reign, Puritan nonconformity and Catholic recusancy. His eucharistic doctrine is a finely expressed receptionism, as in his paraphrase of Christ's words of institution, 'This is my Body':

> This hallowed food, through concurrence of divine power, is in verity and truth, unto faithful receivers,

125

> instrumentally a cause of that mystical participation, whereby as I make myself wholly theirs, so I give them in hand an actual possession of all such saving grace as my sacrificed body can yield, and as their souls do presently need, that is to them and in them my body.[3]

Accordingly, the real presence of Christ's body and blood is 'not to be sought for in the sacrament', but rather in 'the worthy receiver of the sacrament'.[4] Hooker attached little importance to the notion of eucharistic sacrifice: the Eucharist, as an offering of praise, may be termed metaphorically a sacrificial act 'although it have properly now no sacrifice'.[5] Metaphor for Hooker is losing, evidently, its ontological foundation.[6]

After Hooker, the seventeenth-century Church of England gave ecclesiastical living room to three parties where eucharistic doctrine was concerned.[7] A central group were receptionists, who held that Christ is spiritually present whenever the consecrated elements are received in faith. Such men were, in their general theological outlook, Calvinists of a moderate hue. To their left stood those with a Zwinglian doctrine: these were, in wider terms, Latitudinarians who would come increasingly to dominate the Church after the Glorious Revolution of 1688. To their right, finally, we find the high churchmen: trembling on the brink of the Catholic doctrines of the sacrifice and the presence, they were restrained by a fear of Romanising at once political, theological and instinctive.

After the restoration of the Church of England in 1660 (following a period of proscription under the Presbyterian 'Commonwealth' and the Independentist 'Protectorate'), a projected reform of the eucharistic rite of the Book of Common Prayer could have introduced greater clarity. But fear of alienating those Protestant dissenters who might be brought, however grudgingly, to accept the Restoration settlement meant that the attempt of 1662 was somewhat fudged. The rubrics were modified in a Catholic direction; the prayers, by contrast, remained virtually untouched. Thus a rudimentary offertory rite was added, as also a fraction, while the idea of consecration was restored and, with it, the practice of consuming the remains of the consecrated elements. But Cranmer's prayers now required a strained interpretation indeed if they were to cover this enriched conception of what it is that is done at the Eucharist.[8]

The mantle of the high churchmen, potent as these were in the making of the 1662 liturgy, would fall, with the coming of the Dutchman William III and his co-sovereign Mary II, onto the shoulders of the Non-Jurors. Owing to their belief in the 'divine right' of a duly crowned and anointed king, these churchmen would not accept the parliamentary removal of the Stuart James II in 1688, and broke communion with the rest of the Church of England on this point. Though influential for a while in Scotland, where Anglicanism did not form the State Church, they disappear from the scene after the failure of their attempt to enter into communion with the Eastern Orthodox.[9] However, the adoption, by many Non-Jurors, of a new Communion Office, based partly on the primitive liturgies know to them and partly on the first Prayer Book of Edward VI (1549), and typified by the adoption of such customs as the mixed chalice, prayer of the departed, and, most importantly, an oblatory prayer offering the elements to the Father as symbols of Christ's body and blood, together with an *epiklêsis*, calling down the Holy Spirit upon the consecrated elements, foreshadowed the ritual reforms desiderated by the later Tractarians.

The eighteenth-century episcopate was almost entirely Latitudinarian, yet from the small pool of high churchmen there came the massively influential Evangelical movement of John and Charles Wesley. It is a paradox of English Church history that it was the high-church wing of the Evangelical revival, the wing of the Wesleys, which eventually broke away from Anglicanism. The eucharistic doctrine of the Wesleys' splendid hymns verges on the Catholic,[10] but in both theology and devotion had little influence on those who remained within the national church as Anglican Evangelicals.

127

Writing on the eve of the Evangelical revival, Archdeacon
Daniel Waterland (1683-1740) revived the receptionist
doctrine of the Eucharistic gifts, and the concept of the
Eucharist as a spiritual sacrifice, characteristic, if anything
be, of Anglicanism's 'central churchmanship'.[11] In his *Review
of the Doctrine of the Eucharist as Laid Down in Scripture and
Antiquity* Waterland evidently felt obliged, however, to come
to some view of the consecrated elements as such.[12] He asks,
therefore, what relationship the elements may have to the
body and blood of Christ, and, in answering his own question,
draws an analogy from the surprisingly selected realm of
mediaeval property law. The eucharistic elements are like
the ring or crozier of a bishop, used to convey, by investiture,
a right, privilege and office. So, for Waterland, the bread
and wine, after consecration, are 'called by the names of
what they are pledges of and are ordained to convey'.[13] In
The Christian Sacrifice Explained, one of his 'Charges' to the
Middlesex clergy, Waterland speaks of the Eucharist as a
spiritual sacrifice which secures for us the benefits of Christ's
death as the sole ground of our acceptance by God. But
he was deeply suspicious of any suggestion that Christ still
pleads his sacrifice before the Throne in heaven — and *a
fortiori* of the notion that the Church, in the Eucharist, unites
herself with that pleading, for this was held to detract from
the once-for-all character of the sacrifice on Calvary, termed
by Evangelicals 'Christ's finished work'. Waterland's
writings on the Eucharist were republished in the mid-
nineteenth century with the hope of countering the rising
party of the Anglo-Catholics, the successors to the
Tractarians, or Oxford Movement men, of the 1830s.

Like the seventeenth-century high churchmen, whom they
so revered, the Tractarians appealed to the witness of the
Church Fathers, but increasingly — and with the Anglo-
Catholics overwhelmingly — they lost the inhibitions of
the Caroline and Restoration divines about following through
the logic of that appeal. If a doctrine stood proved by the

testimony of Scripture and the Fathers, it would not worry them to find that it was also taught by the Church of Rome. Although they avoided the term trans-substantiation, they held firmly to the doctrine of the objective presence of Christ's body and blood which is its ground. Similarly, they defended the doctrine of eucharistic sacrifice, and worked hard to clear it of the charge that it entailed a depreciation of the sacrifice of the Cross.[14] The Tractarians' successors, the Anglo-Catholics, rightly perceiving that assent to such doctrines could not leave liturgical and devotional practice unaffected, sponsored a revival of Catholic ritual and sacramental spirituality, notably through the 'slum parishes' of Victorian London and the industrial towns.[15]

From this summary sketch it may appear that the chief difficulty faced by the first Anglican Roman Catholic International Commission (ARCIC I) was not so much how to unite Roman Catholics with Anglicans, as how to unite Anglican Evangelicals with Anglican Catholics! The relegation of the term trans-substantiation to the status of a footnote is symptomatic of this. As we have seen, the issue of trans-substantiation did not particularly interest Anglican high churchmen, partly because, like nearly all Anglican theologians of the relevant periods, they lacked a developed interest in a Christian metaphysics. By contrast, trans-substantiation is a major theme, as this book has shown, in Roman Catholic doctrinal formularies, not least because of the enduring concern for a (to be sure, soteriologically subordinated) ontology which, in the crucial instance of Christology, is as ancient, in the Great Church, as the Creed of Nicaea itself.[16]

It is a by no means implausible interpretation of the text of ARCIC I on the Eucharist to say that, in its negotiation, Roman Catholics utilised their own resources of recent scholarship to assist Anglican Catholics and Anglican Evangelicals to reach a degree of common ground. This took place through the agency of two concepts in particular: those of the eucharistic sacrifice as an effective memorial (*anamnêsis*), and of the consecrated elements as the real but spiritual presence of Christ.

The teaching of ARCIC I that the Eucharist constitutes an effective memorial of Christ's sacrifice marks a significant advance on the positions of the past. Representatives of both 'extremes' of Anglicanism agreed that the Eucharist is the sacramental expression of Christ's sacrifice on Calvary. However, we must note that the text is not especially clear as to what the effect of the effective memorial may be. Is it actually to make present the sacrifice of Christ, or is it simply the gracious power to make us remember that sacrifice in a way which works unto salvation? The biblical term, *anamnêsis*, has a certain vagueness which permits this ambiguity. Dr Graham Leonard, the Anglican bishop of London, has written of the passage concerned:

> It may be noted in passing that there is not a single word in this section to indicate that the memorial is effected in a sacramental way. Except for the reference to the fact that the Eucharist was instituted by Christ, the section could be descriptive of the proclamation of God's reconciling acts by the ministry of the Word. . .

And Leonard concludes:

> It does seem extraordinary to base the central idea of the Eucharist concerning the manner in which the Church is enabled to participate in and benefit from the Lord's saving acts upon the debatable meaning of one word instead of discussing the nature of the unique mode of sacramental signification.[17]

The force of Dr Leonard's remarks is particularly apparent when one considers the evident reluctance of the text to pick up the Tridentine concern for the Mass as a sacrifice not only of praise but also of propitiation (since its Victim is the slaughtered Lamb). This is a point on which Evangelicals may be expected to show an especial reserve.

The other key concept in ARCIC I is the notion that the consecrated elements are the real, if spiritual — that is, non-natural — presence of Jesus Christ. Objection may be taken to the use of the word 'spiritual' in this context as tending to reduce the force of the other chief adjective, 'real'. A better indicator of the non-natural character of the presence, for this reason, would be the phrase 'real, if sacramental'. Yet the terms of the text, once again, register true progress when read against the historical background. Insofar as there is such a thing as a mainstream tradition of Anglican eucharistic thinking, that mainstream would be for one major commentator, receptionist rather than realist, in force. The late R.P.C. Hanson, formerly Bishop of Clogher in the (Anglican) Church of Ireland, and afterwards professor of theology in the University of Manchester, remarked of the idea of an identification of the consecrated elements with the Lord's body and blood (which belief in a real, if spiritual, presence evidently entails):

> It is even doubtful whether this can be described as formal Anglican doctrine. Of course it must not be thought to be contrary to Anglican doctrine, and for some considerable time now many Anglicans have believed this doctrine in some sense. But on the whole it has been the Anglican tradition not to take this further step, i.e. not to say that the bread and wine are not Christ's body and blood, but not to say that they are.

And with, perhaps, a touch of exaggeration, Hanson went on:

> The Anglican doctrine since the end of the sixteenth century at the latest has consistently been that the consecrated elements convey — are the vehicles of — Christ's body and blood, in such a way that he who partakes in faith receives Christ's body and blood, and he who does not partake, or who does not partake in faith, does not thus sacramentally receive Christ's body and blood.

131

If challenged further as to what 'receiving Christ's body and blood' means, then, Hanson assures us:

> the great majority of Anglican theologians and of Anglican communicants would say that it means being made sharers in Christ's life.[18]

The difficulty of the text, for the Catholic reader who does not wish to be thought ungrateful for the steps taken thus officially by Anglicans (with varying degrees of enthusiasm) towards the Catholic position, lies in its reluctance to enter upon either the salvific ontology of the real presence or the question of the practical implications of that presence for such matters as the cultus of the Reserved Sacrament.[19]

This reluctance follows in some wise inevitably from the method used by ARCIC I in its deliberations. For the Commission chose not to compare the existing formularies and practices of the churches but to go back, behind such affirmations and deportment, to their biblical and patristic roots. It was this approach by way of *ressourcement* which enabled some important advances to be made, but, at the same time, that approach disqualified the Commission from doing justice to the post-patristic developments. It may be said that, in this respect, the teaching of ARCIC I is actually a representation in modern ecumenical idiom of the position of the seventeenth-century high churchmen who looked precisely to the Bible and the Fathers over against the Middle Ages and Catholic Reformation, and the contemporary practice of Rome.[20]

Notes

Chapter 1: The Eucharist in the New Testament

1. R.E. Brown SS, 'The Johannine Sacramentary Re-considered', *Theological Studies* 23 (1962), pp. 183–206.
2. R. Bultmann, *Das Evangelium des Johannes* (Göttingen 1941).
3. R.E. Brown, SS, *The Gospel according to John, i-xii* (New York 1966), pp. cxi–cxiv.
4. C. Ruch, L'Eucharistie d'après la Sainte Ecriture', *Dictionnaire de Théologie Catholique* V.1 (Paris 1913; 1939), col. 991.
5. *Didache* 9; 10.
6. On the feeding miracles as the eschatological counterpart of Moses and the manna, see A. Heising, *Die Botschaft der Brotvermehrung* (Stuttgart 1966).
7. (Syriac) *Apocalypse of Baruch* 29, 8.
8. *Midrash Qoheleth* I. 9, cited G. Wainwright, *Eucharist and Eschatology* (London 1971), p. 22.
9. John 6, 32b. Psalm 77, indeed, has seen in the manna 'bread of heaven, of angels'; Christian tradition, in the light of this gospel, will transfer these phrases to the eucharistic food.
10. John 6:35.
11. Proverbs 9:5.
12. John 4:32–34.
13. Ibid. 8:56–58.
14. Ibid. 6:61.
15. Ibid. 6:63.
16. A. Loisy, *Le quatrième Evangile* (Paris 1921), p. 704.
17. 1 Corinthians 11:29.
18. John 17:19.
19. A. Loisy, *Le quatrième Evangile*, op. cit., p. 815.
20. John 19:32–37.
21. Ibid. 7:38–39.
22. *Mishnah Talmud* 4, 2.
23. C. Ruch, 'L'Eucharistie d'après la Sainte Ecriture', art. cit., col. 1010.
24. I.e. verses 25, 29. The whole 'Hallel'consisted of Psalms 113–118.
25. Described in a highly circumstantial and fascinating way by J. Jeremias, *The Eucharistic Words of Jesus* (ET London 1966).
26. John 18:28.
27. Ibid. 19:14.
28. A. Jaubert, *la Date de la Cène* (Paris 1957); idem. 'Jésus et le calendrier de Qumran', *New Testament Studies* 7. 1 (1960), pp. 1–30.
29. J. Mahoney, 'The Last Supper and the Qumran Calendar', *Clergy Review* NS 48. 6 (1963), p. 226.
30. Some support for this in Philo, *Vita Moysis* 2, 224, cited by A. Jaubert, op. cit., p. 23.

31. C. Ruch, 'L'Eucharistie d'après la Sainte Ecriture', art. cit., col. 1035.
32. Matthew 26:28.
33. Cf. G. Wainwright, *Eucharist and Eschatology*, op. cit., pp.22-23, and, much more fully, R. Le Déaut, *La Nuit pascale* (Rome 1963).
34. 1 Corinthians 10:16.
35. Ibid. 11:23.
36. See on this the epoch-making M. Thurian, *L'Eucharistie. Mémorial du Seigneur, sacrifice d'action de grâce et d'intercession* (Neuchâtel 1959).
37. 1 Corinthians 11:25.
38. Ibid. 11:27.
39. Acts of the Apostles 2:42.
40. *Apostolic Tradition* 23, 14; cf. J. Jeremias, *The Eucharistic Words of Jesus*, op. cit., p. 136.
41. *Letters and Diaries* IV. pp. 179-180, cited in I. Ker, *John Henry Newman. A Biography* (Oxford 1989), p. 89; see also R.C. Selby, *The Principle of Reserve in the Writings of John Henry Cardinal Newman* (Oxford 1975).

Chapter 2: The Eucharist in the Age of the Fathers

1. *Commentary on Leviticus* 7, 5.
2. *Egyptian Church Order* (Ethiopic 'Statutes of the Apostles', cited D. Stone, *History of the Doctrine of the Holy Eucharist* (London 1909), I. p. 28. The historical materials in this book are much indebted to this immensely learned Anglo-Catholic scholar.
3. *The Pedagogue* II, 2, 29.
4. *Against Marcion* III, 19; IV, 40; *On Prayer*, 6.
5. A. von Harnack, *Lehrbuch der Dogmengeschichte* (Freiburg 1886-1889; Tübingen 1903; ET, of the third German edition, London 1894-1899), II, p. 144; IV, p. 289.
6. Philippians 2:6.
7. See Cyprian, *Testimonies*, 2, 13; 3, 39.
8. C.H. Turner, *Ecclesiae Occidentalis Monumenta Iuris Antiquissima* (Oxford 1899-1930), I, p. 174.
9. Tertullian, *Apology* 21. For the many instances of *repraesentare/repraesentatio*, see D. Stone, *History of the Doctrine of the Holy Eucharist*, op. cit., I, pp. 31-33.
10. *To the Smyrnaeans* 7, 1.
11. *Apology* I, 66.
12. *Against the Heretics* IV, 18, 5.
13. For the Autun inscription, see H. Leclerq, 'Autun (archéologie)', in F. Cabrol (ed.), *Dictionnaire de Archéologie chrétienne et de Liturgie* I, 1 (Paris 1907), cols. 3195-3198.
14. *On the Shows* 25.
15. *The Chaplet (De corona)* 3.
16. *On Prayer* 19.
17. *Concerning Idolatry* 7.
18. *Letter* 58, 9.
19. Fragments *On Matthew* 7, 6 (P.G. 27, col. 1380).

20. *Sermon* 91, 3.
21. *Catechetical Lectures* 19.
22. Ibid. 22.
23. Ibid. 23.
24. Cf. E.L. Mascall, *Corpus Christi* (London 1953; 1965), p. 259.
25. C. Comment, 'Adoration eucharistique et renouveau liturgique', *Parole et pain* 13 (1966), p. 92.
26. A. Vonier, OSB, 'The Relationship between Mass and Benediction, and Prayers before the Blessed Sacrament Exposed', in idem, *Sketches and Studies in Theology* (London 1940), pp. 107-145; M. de la Taille, SJ, 'The Real Presence and its Sacramental Function', in idem., *The Mystery of Faith and Human Opinion* (London 1930), pp. 207-217.
27. *To Adimantus, Against the Manichees* 12, 3. For a complementary explanation of Augustine's usage, see F. van der Meer, *Augustine the Bishop* (ET London 1961), who explains, p. 312:

> [Augustine] wrote at an epoch when the worship of the body and blood of Christ consisted simply in reverent reception, handling and consumption; at such a time men had not yet adverted to the idea of looking for the factual presence, which can be continually worshipped, behind the signs which they grasped and the means of grace of which they availed themselves. And in consequence the words *figura* and *signum corporis Christi* sound otherwise in their ears than they do now.

See also on this T. Camelot, 'Réalisme et symbolisme dans la doctrine eucharistique de saint Augustin', *Revue des Sciences Philosophiques et Théologiques* 31 (1947), pp. 394-410.

28. *De recta in Deum fide* 5, 6. Nothing is known of this author whose work, extant only in Latin, its translator Rufinus ascribed to Origen who had 'Adamantios' as a further name. But its date is c. 450: E. Prinzivalli, 'Adamanzio', in A. di Berardino (ed.), *Dizionario Patristico e di antichità cristiane* (Casale Monferrato 1983), p. 41.
29. *The Answer-book (Apocriticus)* 3, 23.
30. Cf. R.L.P. Milburn, 'Symbolism and Realism in Post- Nicene Representation of the Eucharist', *Journal of Ecclesiastical History* 8 (1957), pp. 1-16.
31. Acta of the Iconoclast Synod of Hiereia (754), translated in D.J. Sahas, *Icon and Logos: Sources in Eighth Century Iconoclasm* (Toronto 1986). For a helpful account of this theme and its background, see S. Gerö, 'The Eucharistic Doctrine of the Byzantine Iconoclasts and its Sources', *Byzantinische Zeitschrift* 68 (1975). Father Christopher Walter, of the Augustinians of the Assumption, has pointed out that, whereas the Last Supper and the Communion of the Apostles are frequently represented in early Christian art, they subsequently disappear in the Byzantine world until the eleventh century. He suggests that, missing an opportunity to relate the cult of icons to eucharistic worship, Iconophiles may have been reluctant to portray these two moments in the sacred narrative through hostility to the Iconoclast thesis that the consecrated elements were the *only possible* image of Christ:

The Holy Eucharist

A representation of the Last Supper or the Communion of the Apostles in a public place, particularly as the theological capstone of a decorative programme, might have been interpreted as an endorsement of the Iconoclast thesis.

'The Official Imagery of the Byzantine Church', in idem, *Art and Ritual of the Byzantine Church* (London 1982), pp. 188-189.

32. For the full texts of conciliar speeches and decisions, in English translation, see J. Mendham (ed.), *The Seventh General Council, the Second of Nicaea, in which the Worship of Images was Established* (London 1849).
33. Ibid.
34. *On the Orthodox Faith* 4, 13.
35. See on this R. Taft, SJ, *The Great Entrance. A History of the Transfer of Gifts and Other Pre-Anaphora Rites* (Rome 1975). Modern Eastern Orthodox presentations of the Holy Eucharist are much indebted to the 'shape' of the Byzantine liturgy. See, for instance, P. Evdokimov, *La Prière de l'Eglise d'Orient* (Mulhouse 1966); A. Schmemann, *The Eucharist* (Crestwood, New York 1990). In this, they take inspiration from such Byzantine writers as the seventh-century Maximus Confessor and the fourteenth-century Nicholas Cabasilas. On the eucharistic theology of the separated Eastern churches, see T. Spačil, 'Doctrina theologicae Orientis separati de Sanctissima Eucharistia', in *Orientalia Christiania Periodica* 13 (1928), pp. 189-279; 14 (1929), pp. 5-173. For a modern Catholic survey of the eucharistic doctrine implied in the ancient liturgies, see J. Betz, 'Das Zeugnis der Liturgie', in *Eucharistie in der Schrift und Patristik* (Freiburg 1979), pp. 54-67.
36. 'On the Baptism of Christ', P.G. 46, cols. 581-584.
37. D. Stone, *History of the Doctrine of the Holy Eucharist*, op. cit., pp. 98-109.
38. *Eranistes*, dialogue II. P.G. 83, cols. 165-168.
39. *On the Two Natures in Christ* [the ascription of which to Pope Gelasius is disputed], cited D. Stone, *History of the Doctrine of the Holy Eucharist*, I, p. 102.
40. *Catechetical Lectures* 22.
41. *Catechetical Oration.*
42. *On the Betrayal of Judas, and the Pasch* I. 6.
43. *Homilies on Matthew* 82, 5.
44. J.H. McKenna, *Eucharist and Holy Spirit. The Epiclesis in Twentieth Century Theology, 1900-1966* (London 1975), pp. 48-71.
45. *Catechetical Oration.*
46. See especially: *Letter* 17; *Against Nestorius* 4; *Commentary on John*, on 6, 64; *Explanation of the Twelve Chapters* 11, and, more generally, E. Gebremedhin, *Life-giving Blessing. An Inquiry into the Eucharistic Doctrine of Cyril of Alexandria* (Uppsala 1977).
47. H. Chadwick, 'Eucharist and Christology in the Nestorian Controversy', *Journal of Theological Studies* N.S. 2 (1951). Compare the profession of eucharistic faith made by the celebrant in the Coptic liturgy:

> Amen, amen, amen, I believe, I believe and I confess till the last breath that this is the Life-giving flesh which thine only-begotten

136

Son, our Lord and our God and our Saviour, Jesus Christ, took from our Lady and Mistress of us all, the Mother of God, the holy Mary. he made it one with his divinity without mingling and without confusion and without alteration... I believe that his divinity was not separated from his humanity for a single moment, nor for the twinkling of an eye.

Cited W. A. Girgis, *The Christological Teaching of the Non-Chalcedonian Churches* (Cairo 1962), p. 7.

48. *Letter of Barnabas,* 2.
49. *Dialogue* 22; *Against Marcion* 2, 18, 22.
50. *Supplication* 13.
51. *The Miscellanies* 7, 49.
52. *Against the Heresies* IV. 18, 1.
53. E.g. *Didache* 14; Irenaeus, *Against the Heresies* IV. 17, 5; Tertullian, *Against Marcion* 3, 22. Malachi's text is incorporated into the opening of the Egyptian anaphora of St Mark (evidenced as early as the fourth century):

We give thanks and offer thee this spiritual sacrifice, this unbloody worship, offered to thee by all men from the rising of the sun until its setting, from the north to the south, for thy Name is great among all the nations and everywhere is offered to thy Name a pure sacrifice, a sacrifice and oblation.

Cited from A.G. Martimort (ed.), *The Eucharist* (ET Shannon 1973), p. 144.

54. *Dialogue* 70.
55. *Letter* 83.
56. *Against the Heresies* IV. 18.
57. *Homilies on Leviticus* 6, 2; 7, 2; 9: *Homilies on Judges* 7, 2; *On Martyrdom* 30; 39.
58. *Euchologion* 1.
59. *Catechetical Lectures* 23.
60. *On Psalm* 38: *Enarration* 25.
61. The relevant texts are gathered and interpreted in M. Blein, *Le sacrifice de l'Eucharistie d'après Saint Augustin* (Lyons 1906).
62. *On the Burial Ground and the Cross,* 3; and *Homilies on Romans* 8, 8.
63. *Letter* 171.
64. *Homilies on Hebrews* 11, 2-3; *On the Priesthood* 3, 4.
65. *City of God,* X. 3.
66. Ibid. X. 6.
67. Ibid. X. 5.
68. Ibid. X. 6.
69. Ibid.
70. Ibid. X. 20.
71. Ibid.
72. 1 Corinthians 10: 17.
73. Sermon 272. See on this theme, G. Bonner, 'The Church and the Eucharist in the Theology of Saint Augustine', *Sobornost* 7, 6 (Winter 1978), pp. 448-461.

74. *Against the Heretics* V. 33, 1.
75. *Quaestiones Evangelorum* I. 43.
76. *Letter* 120, 2.
77. E.g. Origen, *Exhortation to Martyrdom* 40; Cyprian, *Letter* 63, 9.
78. G. Wainwright, *Eucharist and Eschatology* (London 1971) p. 45.
79. See ibid., pp. 51-56, for a variety of fine texts to this effect.
80. Ibid. p. 52.

Chapter 3: The Mediaevals on the Nature of the Real Presence

1. Cf. Paschasius, *De corpore et sanguine Domini* 1.
2. Ibid. 18.
3. Ratramnus, *De corpore et sanguine Domini* 5.
4. Ibid. 9, 10.
5. Ibid. 7, 8.
6. E.g. ibid. 54.
7. Cited Lanfranc, *De corpore et sanguine Domini* 2.
8. M. Gibson, in her *Lanfranc of Bec* (Oxford 1978), ascribes Lanfranc's motivation to loyalty to the memory of Leo IX and Humbert. But he also represented the 'Norman orthodoxy', which, in the 1050s, had raised up against Berengar his earliest opponents: three monks of the ducal monastery of Fécamp — Abbot John, in his *Confessio fidei*, his cross-bearer Durand of Troarn, and Archbishop Mauritius, convener of a synod which offered a eucharistic confession of faith: ibid. p. 65.
9. *De sacramentis* 43; 54.
10. Lanfranc, *De corpore et sanguine Domini* 18, 19.
11. Now edited by R.B.C. Huygens as *Beringerius Turonensis, Rescriptum contra Lanfrannum* (Turnhout 1988, = *Corpus Christianorum, continuatio medievalis* 84).
12. D.-S. 700: the work of Alberic of Monte Cassino.
13. *Tractates on John,* 26, 18.
14. H. Chadwick, 'Ego Berengarius', *Journal of Theological Studies* NS 40, 2 (1989), p. 434.
15. D. Stone, *History of the Doctrine of the Holy Eucharist,* op. cit. I. p. 258.
16. D.-S. 802.
17. 'Ego Berengarius', art. cit. p. 442.
18. *Summa Theologiae* IIIa., q.75. a.1.
19. Ibid. q.75, a.2.
20. A claim is made to resolve these difficulties, using modern physics, in J.A. O'Driscoll, SM, 'The Reality of the Real Presence', *Downside Review* 93, 312 (July 1975). But the traditional view — for it is echoed in the East by Damascene, *De fide orthodoxa* IV. 13, as it is stated in the West by Thomas, was re-instated by W.M. Gordon who wrote by way of reply:

> The true movement ... in the sacrament is best imagined not by the descent of Christ into countless hosts but by the converging ascent of the many faithful to the one Christ. In such a vision, the laws of the temporal order and mundane existence no longer obtain; measure, distance, speed are not relevant here. These latter calculations belong to this world; the Eucharist belongs to the eschaton, the heavenly,

ultimate, reality. So by explaining Christ's presence through the intervention of motion and velocity we 'reduce to the order of space and time that which is meant to draw us out of it'.

'Time, Space and the Eucharist', *Downside Review* 95. 319 (April 1977), p. 116, with a citation from H.M. Féret, *The Eucharist Today* (ET New York 1968), p.83.

21. *Summa Theologiae*, IIIa., q.75, a.4.
22. Ibid. q.75, a.4, ad iii.
23. Ibid. q.78, a.1.
24. R. F. Buxton, *Eucharist and Institution Narrative. A Study in the Roman and Anglican Traditions of the Consecration of the Eucharist from the Eighth to the Twentieth Centuries* (Great Wakering 1967), pp. 39–40.
25. J.H. McKenna, *Eucharist and Holy Spirit. The Eucharistic Epiclesis in Twentieth Century Theology* (Great Wakering 1975).
26. *Summa Theologiae*, IIIa., q.75, a.1, ad i.
27. Ibid. q.78, a.4, ad i.
28. A. Stolz, OSB, *Manuale Theologiae Dogmaticae, IV. De Sacramentis* (Freiburg 1943), pp. 144–145.
29. *Summa Theologiae* IIIa., q.76, a.7.
30. Ibid. IIIa q.77. a.1.
31. Ibid. IIIa q.77, a.6.
32. Ibid. IIIa., q.76, a.1.
33. Ibid. IIIa., q.76, a.3.
34. Ibid. IIIa., q.76, arts. 5–6.
35. Ibid. IIIa., q.76, a.6.
36. Ibid. IIIa., q.77, a.7.
37. D.-S. 1642.
38. Ibid. 1636; cf. canon 1 on the sacrament of the Eucharist at ibid. 1651.

Chapter 4: The Mediaevals on the Purpose of the Real Presence

1. Thus modifying slightly the terminology preferred by G. Macy, *The Theologies of the Eucharist in the Early Scholastic Period. A Study of the Salvific Function of the Sacrament according to the Theologians c.1080-c.1220* (Oxford 1984) — to which study my account is indebted.
2. Cf. ibid. pp. 44–72, 'The Paschasian Approach to the Eucharist'.
3. *Elucidarium* 1. 83; *Gemma animae* 1. 36.
4. *De sancta Trinitate* 36, 3, 26.
5. *Summa Theologiae* IIIa., q. 73, a. 3.
6. *Letter* 3.
7. *Summa Theologiae* IIIa., q. 79, a. 3.
8. Some comments on the necessity of not divorcing the Holy Eucharist from 'the general field of sacramental vision', in W. Barden, OP, 'The Sacramentality of the Eucharist' in ibid. (ed.) *St Thomas Aquinas. Summa Theologiae. Volume 58, The Eucharistic Presence* (London 1965), pp. 197–200. On the spread of the particular vocabulary explained here as an expression

of the sacramental vision, see J. de Ghellinck, 'Eucharistie au XIIe siècle en Occident', *Dictionnaire de Théologie Catholique* XV. 1, col. 1270.

9. G. Macy, *The Theologies of the Eucharist in the Early Scholastic Period*, op. cit., pp. 76–84.

10. *Summa Theologiae* IIIa., q.80, a.10, with a reference to Ambrose, *De Sacramentis* IV. 6.

11. *Summa Theologiae* IIIa., q.80, a.10, the allusion to Augustine's teaching comes, however, from a sermon whose ascription is not secure, at P.L. 39, col. 1909. Thomas' closing citation is from Gennadius of Marseilles' *Liber ecclesiasticorum dogmatum*, at P.L. 58, 944.

12. G. Macy, *The Theologies of the Eucharist in the Early Scholastic Period*, op. cit., p. 94.

13. *Summa Theologiae* IIIa., q.79, a.1.

14. Ibid. IIIa., q.79, a.2, ad i.

15. Ibid. IIIa., q.79, a.3, Contrary to a widespread later opinion in moral theology, sins of omission are not always voluntary, yet they can be grave. The habitual sinner does not become progressively less blameworthy on the grounds that he does not need explicit voluntary acts to perform evil deeds!

16. Ibid. IIIa., q.79, a.4.

17. See G. Wainwright, *Eucharist and Eschatology* (London 1971), pl 53.

18. G. Macy, *The Theologies of the Eucharist in the Early Scholastic Period*, op. cit. p. 107.

19. H. de Lubac, SJ, *Corpus mysticum. L'Eucharistie et l'Eglise au moyen age* (Paris 1939-1944; 1948), pp. 23-46.

20. Ibid. p. 33.

21. G. Macy, *The Theologies of the Eucharist in the Early Scholastic Period*, op. cit. pp. 112-114.

22. Ibid. pp. 114-118.

23. Ibid. p. 121.

24. *Sententiae* IV. 8, 6-7.

25. J. Hamer, *'L'Eglise est une communion* (Paris 1962), p. 84; cf. the discussion of Thomas' understanding of the inter-relation of Eucharist and Church in J.M. Tillard, *L'Eucharistie, pâques de l'Eglise* (Paris 1964).

Chapter 5: The Eucharistic Sacrifice from Trent to the Nineteenth Century

1. Thomas Aquinas, *Summa Theologiae*, IIIa., q.79, arts. 2 and 5.

2. Peter Lombard, *The Sentences* IV. 12, 7.

3. G. Biel, *Sacri canonis missae expositio resolutissima, litteralis ac mystica* (Basle 1910); on his teaching: P. Anatriello, *La dottrina di Gabriele Biel sull'Eucaristia* (Milan 1937).

4. See especially Luther's *Concerning the Babylonish Captivity of the Church* (1519), where the three 'bondages' listed are: communion under one kind, transubstantiation as a dogma of faith (and not simply a human opinion), and the Mass as a sacrifice or good work; see E. Iserloh, *Der Kampf um die Messe in den ersten Jahren der Auseinandersetzung mit Luther* (Marburg 1952).

5. G. Biel, *Sacri canonis missae expositiom . . . Lectio* 85.
6. A claim maintained in the *Augsburg Confession* (1530). In the 1551 *Wurtemberg Confession*, however, the Eucharist is allowed to be a sacrifice in a general sense, since, at least when celebrated in the context of preaching the Word of God, and where its benefits are understood as received through faith, it is a memorial of Christ's death and a means of applying the merits of his Passion to the communicants.
7. F. Clark, SJ, *The Eucharistic Sacrifice and the Reformation* (London 1960), pp. 469-503. The writings of Catherinus (Lancelot Politi) were, so Darwell Stone comments, 'somewhat eccentric': Cano, Vasquez and Suarez, the great Iberian Scholastics of his day, all thought he had limited the saving efficacy of the Cross to pre-baptismal sins, yet other passages in his work suggest otherwise: *A History of the Doctrine of the Holy Eucharist* (London 1909), II, pp. 70-75.
8. Albert Pighius, 'On the Sacrifice of the Mass', cited D. Stone, *A History of the Doctrine of the Holy Eucharist* op. cit., II. p. 70.
9. D.-S. 1740.
10. Ibid. 1753.
11. D. Power, *The Sacrifice We Offer. The Tridentine Dogma and its Reinterpretation* (Edinburgh 1987), p. 128.
12. Melchior Cano, *De locis theologicis,* XII, 11.
13. D. Stone, *A History of the Doctrine of the Holy Eucharist,* op. cit., II. pp. 359-373.
14. John de Lugo, *De venerabili Eucharistiae sacrificio, disputatio* 19, 5.
15. J.C. Hedley, OSB, *The Holy Eucharist* (London 1907), pp. 159-160. The allusion is to Gregory's Letter 171, to Amphilochius of Iconium.
16. A. Nichols, OP, 'Homage to Scheeben, 1888-1988', *The Month* 249, 1452 (1988), pp. 1028-1031.
17. M.J. Scheeben, *The Mysteries of Christianity* (ET St Louis, Missouri and London 1947), p. 510.
18. Not unconnected with the spirituality of 'abandonment to divine Providence', *abandon,* whose master is the French Jesuit Jean-Pierre de Caussade.
19. Thalhofer's importance for the exposition of a theology of sacrifice as surrender is underlined in M. Lepin, *L'Idée du sacrifice de la Messe d'après les théologiens depuis les origines jusqu'à nos jours* (Paris 1926). Thalhofer's *Das Opfer des Alten und Neuen Bundes* (Regensburg 1870), is cited here at p. 214.
20. Ibid. p. 263.
21. See J. Galy, *La sacrifice dans l'Ecole Française* (Paris 1951).
22. C. de Condren, *L'Idée du sacerdoce et sacrifice de Jésus Christ* (Paris 1677), I. 8.
23. Ibid. I. 9.
24. J.J. Olier, *Traité des saints Ordres* (reprinted Paris 1856), III. 5. However, the *Explication des Cérémonies de la Grande Messe paroissiale,* also republished at Paris in that year as part of the *Oeuvres complètes* edited by the indefatigable J. P. Migne, has a more careful formulation of the same teaching. See P. Michalon, *La communion chez les mystères de Jésus-Christ selon Jean-Jacques Olier* (Lyons 1943).

25. A. Nichols, OP, *The Art of God Incarnate. Theology and Image in Christian Tradition* (London 1980), pp. 65–66; for a full account, S. Gerö, 'Eusebius' Letter to Constania Reconsidered', *Journal of Theological Studies* N. S. 32 (1981), pp. 460–470.

26. For Marcellus: C. Kannengiesser, 'Marcello di Ancyra', in A. di Berardino (ed.), *Dizionario Patristico e di Antichità Cristiane* (Casale Monferrato 1984), II. cols. 2089–2091.

27. C. de Condren, *Perfection de l'immolation et de l'inflammation dans le Ciel*, II. 26.

28. A very full account in J. Carreyre, 'Pistoie (Synode de)', *Dictionnaire de Théologie Catholique* XII. 2, cols. 2134–2229.

29. D.-S. 2630.

30. D. Stone, *A History of the Doctrine of the Holy Eucharist*, op. cit., II. pp. 409–411.

31. See on this Paul VI's instruction of 1974 *Firma in traditione* which, in Father Edward Kilmartin's summary, sees the Eucharist as

    > A sacrifice of almsgiving by which the faithful more intimately associate themselves with Christ offering himself as victim, and as an expression of their fellowship with the priest who exercises his ministry on their behalf.

    — in M. Searle (ed.), *Liturgy and Social Justice* (Collegeville, Minnesota 1980), p. 65. The fullest study of this subject is K.J. Merk, *Das Mess-stipendium, geschichtlich, dogmatisch, rechtlich und aszetisch erklärt* (Stuttgart 1929); whose main conclusions were offered more briefly beforehand by the same author in *Abriss einer liturgiegeschichtlichen Darstellung des Mess-stipendiums* (Stuttgart 1928).

Chapter 6: Catholic Eucharistic Theology in the Twentieth-Century

1. A. Vonier, OSB, *A Key to the Doctrine of the Eucharist* (London 1925); reprinted in *Collected Works II* (London 1952), pp. 229–360.

2. M. de la Taille, *The Mystery of Faith* (ET London 1941–1950).

3. Ibid. I. p. 43.

4. Ibid. I. pp. 39–46; 50–74.

5. Ibid. I. p. 74.

6. Ibid. I. p. 140.

7. H. Grisewood (ed.), *Epoch and Artist. Selected Writings by David Jones* (London 1959), p. 168.

8. In R. Hague (ed.), *Dai Greatcoat. A Self-portrait of David Jones in his Letters* (London 1980), pp. 231–232.

9. H. Grisewood (ed.) *Epoch and Artist*, op. cit., pp. 168–169. See especially the opening and closing section of Jones' *Anathemata*: 'Rite and Fore-time' and 'Sherthursdaye and Venus Day'. Jones' debt to De la Taille in these passages is brought out by René Hague in his *A Commentary on the 'Anathemata' of David Jones* (Wellingborough 1977), especially p. 4:

    > Maurice de la Taille was the first person whose name came from

David's pen when he acknowledged his debt to a long list of living or recently living authors.... The very scheme upon which the Anathemata is built is derived from De la Taille's presentation of the Last Supper and Calvary.

10. J. Simon, OSB, 'L'Eucharistie, sacrament de l'unité', *Revue Thomiste* 20 (1912), pp. 583-584.

11. *Lumen Gentium* 3; 7; 11.

12. References to the work of these men will be found in my *Theology in the Russian Diaspora. Church, Fathers, Eucharist in Nikolai Afanas'ev, 1891-1966* (Cambridge 1989), chapter 6.

13. The original (French) text in *Irénikon* 55 (1982).

14. K. Rahner, 'Die vielen Messen und das eine Opfer', *Zeitschrift für Katholische Theologie* 71 (1949), pp. 257-317.

15. The Pope appears to have responded, implicitly, to Rahner's intervention in an address of 2 November 1954 to bishops gathered for the introduction of the feast of the Queenship of Mary. Rahner renewed, and refined, his original article in 'Die vielen Messen als die vielen Opfer Christi', idem. 77 (1955), pp. 94-101. For an English translation of this material, see K. Rahner and A. Häussling, *The Celebration of the Eucharist* (ET London 1968).

16. C. O'Neill, OP, *New Approaches to the Eucharist* (Dublin 1967), pp. 30-31.

17. Ibid. p. 38. The view, this, of Thomas, Scotus, Bellarmine, so De la Taille reported, writing, 'A sacrifice is not only the victim — it is the offering of the victim', *L'oecuménicité du fruit de la Messe: intercession eucharistique et dissidence* (Rome 1926), p. 135.

18. *Mediator Dei*, 101.

19. C. O'Neill, OP, *New Approaches to the Eucharist*, op. cit., p. 51; cf. from an Anglo-Catholic standpoint some words of E. L.Mascall:

> It is indeed good that, at the celebration of the Divine Liturgy, the faithful should be present in number, each one taking his or her part intelligently in the great Eucharistic action... But it must not be forgotten — as I am afraid in certain 'liturgical' circles it has been — that the Liturgy is corporate not because of the numbers or enthusiasm of a congregation in a particular building at a particular time, but because, whether the faithful who are physically present be many or few, it is the act of the great High Priest, acting through and in and for his Mystical Body.
>
> *Christ, the Christian and the Church* (London 1946), p. 197.

20. E. Schillebeeckx, OP, *The Eucharist* (ET London 1968); cf. idem., 'Transubstantiation, Transfinalisation, Transsignification', *Worship* 40, 6 (1966).

21. F. Leenhardt, *Ceci est mon Corps* (Neuchâtel 1955): see F. Clark, SJ, *A 'New Theology' of the Real Presence?* (London 1967, = Catholic Truth Society Document 396), p. 6.

22. C. O'Neill, OP, *New Approaches to the Eucharist*, op. cit.

23. F. Clark, SJ, *A 'New Theology' of the Real Presence?*, op. cit., p. 6.

24. L. Smits, OFM Cap., *Actuele vragen rondom de transsubstantiatie en de tegenwoordigheid des Heren in de H. Eucharistie* (Roermond 1965).

25. C. O'Neill, OP, *New Approaches to the Eucharist*, op. cit., pp. 82–88.
26. *Mysterium fidei*, 146.
27. C. O'Neill, OP, *New Approaches to the Eucharist*, op. cit., pp. 104–110.
28. G. Gutiérrez, *A Theology of Liberation* (ET London 1974; 1983), pp. 262–265. More discussion would have helped here on the relation between the inner-ecclesial brotherhood of the household of faith, at issue in the biblical texts, and a wider extra-ecclesial solidarity.
29. In the most recent Spanish edition of this work, that of 1988, these passages on 'class warfare' are considerably modified into an account of 'social conflict'.
30. *Instruction on Certain Aspects of the 'Theology of Liberation'*, X. 16.
31. *Homilies* 50, 3–4; this text is read in the Roman Liturgy of the Hours for Saturday of the Twenty-First Week of the Year.
32. E. J. Kilmartin, SJ, 'The Sacrifice of Thanksgiving and Social Justice', in M. Searle (ed.), *Liturgy and Social Justice* (ET Collegeville, Minnesota 1980), p. 68. St Thomas' account of the collection is not so different from Kilmartin's initial wider statement:

> The oblations which the people offer to God are under the care of the priests, not only so that they may use them themselves, but also so that they might distribute them faithfully. Partly by using them for the objects needed for divine worship, partly for things needed for the priest's own livelihood — because, as it says (1 Corinthians 10:18), 'those who serve the altar should share with the altar', and partly to be given to the poor, who ought to be cared for in so far as possible from the goods of the Church, because the Lord had a purse for the poor, as Jerome says in his *Commentary on Matthew*.

    Summa Theologiae IIIa., q.86, a.2, with a reference to Jerome, *Super Matthaeum* III, on Matthew 17:28.
33. F.X. Meehan, *A Contemporary Social Spirituality* (Maryknoll, New York 1982), pp. 39–46.

Chapter 7: A Systematic Summary: Balthasar and John Paul II

1. G. Cavallini (ed.), *S. Caterina da Siena. Le Orazioni* (Rome 1978), *orazione* XX, pp. 22–23.
2. For a Thomist presentation — in an idiom, then, related to Catherine's own, see M. V. Bernadot, OP, *The Eucharist and the Trinity* (ET Wilmington, Delaware 1977).
3. J. Saward, *The Mysteries of March. Hans Urs von Balthasar on the Incarnation and Easter* (London 1990), p.88, with a reference to Von Balthasar's *New Elucidations* (ET San Francisco 1986), p.115.
4. J. Saward, *The Mysteries of March*, op. cit., p.89.
5. H. U. von Balthasar, *Elucidations* (ET London 1975), p. 120. Despite his prolific output, Balthasar wrote no book on the Eucharist — because of his palpable desire to integrate its motifs into his theology as a whole. His longest sustained discussion is, perhaps: 'Die Messe: ein Opfer der Kirche', *Spiritus Creator* (Einsiedeln 1967), pp. 166–217.

Notes

6. John Paul II, *Eucharisticum Mysterium* (= Catholic Truth Society Document 519, 'The Holy Eucharist', London 1980).
7. Ibid. 4, pp. 11–12.
8. Ibid. 4, pp. 12–13.
9. Ibid. 7, p. 21.

Appendix: The Eucharist in Anglicanism

1. G. Dix, *The Shape of the Liturgy* (London 1945; 1982), pp. 640–674. For the argument after Dix's death: P. Brooks, *Thomas Cranmer's Doctrine of the Eucharist: An Essay in Historical Development* (New York 1965); C.C. Richardson, 'Cranmer and the Analysis of Eucharistic Doctrine', *Journal of Theological Studies* N.S. 16 (1965), pp. 421–437.
2. 'The body of Christ is given, taken and eaten in the Supper only after an heavenly and spiritual manner': but what is 'given' exists, then, in the sacrament: so H.E. Symonds, *The Council of Trent and the Anglican Formularies* (Oxford 1933), p. 44.
3. *Of the Laws of Ecclesiastical Polity* V. 67, 12.
4. Ibid., v. 67, 6ff. J.E. Booty, 'Hooker's Understanding of the Presence of Christ in the Eucharist', in idem., ed., *The Divine Drama in History and Liturgy* (Allison Park, Pennsylvania 1984), pp. 131–148.
5. R. Hooker, *Of the Laws of Ecclesiastical Polity* V. 78, 2; cf. V. 67, 12.
6. Contrast R. Williams, *Eucharistic Sacrifice – the Roots of a Metaphor* (Bramcote 1982). But this approach (from an Anglican writer) could only be reconciled with the insistence of Trent that the Eucharist is a real sacrifice by an account of metaphor which allowed the latter to make ontological commitments on our behalf, as in, for example, C. Ernst, OP, 'Metaphor and Ontology in *Sacra Doctrina*', *The Thomist* (1974), republished in idem., *Multiple Echo. Explorations in Theology* (London 1979), pp. 57–75.
7. C. W. Dugmore, *Eucharistic Doctrine in England from Hooker to Waterland* (London 1942), pp. 30–110.
8. H. Green, 'The Eucharist in Anglican Controversy', *Sobornost* 3, 18 (winter 1955–1956), pp. 288–289.
9. See H. W. Langford, 'The Non-Jurors and the Eastern Orthodox', *Eastern Churches Review* 2 (1967), pp. 118–131, who points out, relevantly for our purposes here:

> The Non-Juror bishops showed in their correspondence a strong reluctance to 'go behind' the English Reformation Settlement, and were obviously very ill at ease in dealing with Orthodox belief on such subjects as transubstantiation and invocation of saints, p. 120.

Apparently influenced by John Johnson's *The Unbloody Sacrifice and Altar Unveiled and Supported* (London 1715), the work of a 'juring' high churchman, the Non-Jurors repudiated the doctrine of a substantial presence and sacrifice of some kind. At a time when the Orthodox East was on the alert for Protestant infiltration their reserves were not well received: the patriarchs called not only the Non-Jurors' denial of transubstantiation, but even

145

criticism or hesitation, blasphemous. During the Oxford Movement, Johnson's work was re-published (Oxford 1847), presumably because of its affirmation that the (spiritual) presence of Christ's body and blood makes possible a representative offering (i.e. the sacramental sacrifice) to the Father.

10. J. E. Rattenbury, *The Eucharistic Hymns of John and Charles Wesley* (London 1945). The author shows the indebtedness of the hymns to the high-church eucharistic doctrine of Daniel Brevint's *The Christian Sacrament and Sacrifice*.

11. C.W. Dugmore's favoured phrase for Waterland in his *Eucharistic Doctrine in England from Hooker to Waterland*, op. cit. As the title suggests, Waterland constitutes, in the author's eyes, the unsurpassable climax of a story.

12. Cambridge 1737, reprinted Oxford 1868 and 1896.

13. Ibid. p. 146.

14. A. Härderlin, *The Tractarian Understanding of the Eucharist* (Uppsala 1965).

15. G. Rowell, 'Pioneers in the Parish: Ritualism in the Slums', in idem., *The Vision Glorious. Themes and Personalities of the Catholic Revival in Anglicanism* (Oxford 1983), pp. 116-140.

16. Cf. P.-L. Carlé, OP, *Consubstantiel et Transsubstantiation* (Bordeaux 1974).

17. Cited from J. Lawrence et al., *A Critique of Eucharistic Agreement* (London 1975), p. 45. Starting from the same notion of memorial, a fuller doctrine is arrived at by the (then) Reformed writer M. Thurian in his *L'Eucharistie* where he sums up his position:

> The Cross is a unique sacrifice in the order of expiation, of reconciliation and of redemption. The Eucharist is a sacramental sacrifice in the order of the application of salvation (the remission of sins) founded upon the unique expiation, of communion founded upon the unique reconciliation, and of intercession founded upon the unique redemption. The Eucharist, the sacrament of the unique sacrifice of the Cross, applies to each individual the salvation (remission of sins) obtained once and for all through Christ's act of expiation; it maintains the communion between God and men, re-established once and for all by Christ's act of reconciliation, and it unites the intercession of the Church with the intercession of Christ in heaven, inaugurated once and for all, by Christ's redemptive act.

L'Eucharistie. Mémorial du Seigneur, sacrifice d'action de grâce et d'intercession (Neuchâtel-Paris 1959); ET *The Eucharistic Memorial* (London 1960), p. 225.

18. Cited from J. Lawrence et al., *A Critique of Eucharistic Agreement*, op.cit., p. 29.

19. On the question of eucharistic ontology, F.W. Temple, the war-time Archbishop of Canterbury, considered that the Church of England 'most wisely refrains' from making any declaration about it.

> By its repudiation of transubstantiation it declares that the Bread when consecrated is still Bread; it refuses to determine the philosophical question whether, in virtue of its new significance as an 'effectual sign' (the phrase of the Articles) or 'instrumental cause' (the phrase of Hooker), it is to be regarded as in any way changed in itself or not.

Temple stressed that it is the significance of the consecrated elements (when received in holy communion) which is of religious importance — and on that, he maintained, 'there is very little dispute among members of the Church of England', cited F. Iremonger, *William Temple, Archbishop of Canterbury. His Life and Letters* (London 1948), pp. 350-351. The question is whether meaning and being can be thus sharply divided.

20. Claimed explicitly by the former Anglican bishop of Leicester, R.R. Williams, in his contribution to J. Lawrence et al., *A Critique of Eucharistic Agreement*, op. cit., pp. 17-18. An apposite example concerns the ARCIC signatories' preference for the language of 'spiritual' presence. John Overall (1560-1619), the probable author of the Anglican *Catechism* of 1604, speaks of the 'whole Christ communicated in the communion of the sacrament':

> not in a carnal, gross, earthly way by transubstantiation or consubstantiation, or any like fictions of human reason, but in a way mystical, heavenly and spiritual, as is rightly laid down in our Articles.

Cited from his *Praelectiones seu Disputationes de Patrum et Christi anima et de Antichristo* in C.W. Dugmore, *Eucharistic Doctrine in England from Hooker to Waterland*, op. cit., p. 40.

Bibliography

A. Origins

P. Benoit, 'Les récits de l'institution et leur portée', *Lumière et vie* 31 (1957), pp. 49-76.

B. Cooke, 'The Synoptic Presentation of the Eucharist as Covenant Sacrifice', *Theological Studies* 21, 1 (1960), pp. 48-49.

J. Delorme et al., *The Eucharist in the New Testament* (London 1964).

T.W. Guzie, *Jesus and the Eucharist* (New York 1974).

J. Jeremias, *The Eucharistic Words of Jesus* (London 1955).

H. Marshall, *Last Supper and Lord's Supper* (London 1984).

C. Ruch, L'Eucharistie d'après la Sainte Ecriture', *Dictionnaire de Théologie Catholique* V.1 (Paris 1913; 1939).

G.S. Sloyan, 'Primitive and Pauline Concepts of the Eucharist', *Catholic Biblical Quarterly* (1961), pp. 1-13.

B. Development

1. General

D. Stone, *A History of the Doctrine of the Holy Eucharist* (London 1909, two volumes). I am much indebted to this classic of Anglo-Catholic scholarship. On its author, see F. L Cross, *Darwell Stone* (Westminster 1943); on his own eucharistic doctrine, pp. 64-73; the bibliography contains references to Stone's other writings, still valuable, not least to (Roman) Catholics, on the eucharistic sacrifice, holy communion and the reserved sacrament. I am glad to report that an English Dominican predecessor, the late Father Victor White, did Stone's *History* appreciative justice in *Blackfriars* (April 1941, pp. 191-194.

M. Lepin, *L'Idée du sacrifice de la Messe d'aprés les théologiens depuis l'origine jusqu'a nos jours* (Paris 1926).

2. Patristic

P. Batiffol, *L'Eucharistie. Etudes d'histoire et de théologie positive* (Paris).

J. Betz, *Eucharistie in der Schrift und Patristik* (Freiburg 1979).

R. J. Daly, *The Origins of the Christian Doctrine of Sacrifice* (Philadelphia 1978).

J. de Walleville, *Le Sacrifice dans les textes eucharistiques des premiers siècles* (Paris 1966).

R. J. Halliburton, 'The Patristic Theology of the Eucharist', in C. Jones et al. (eds.), *The Study of the Liturgy* (London 1978).

H. Jorissen, *Die Entfaltung der Transubstantionslehre bis zum Beginn der Hochscholastik* (Münster 1965).

E. Kilmartin, *The Eucharist in the Primitive Church* (New York 1965).

D. J. Sheenan, *The Eucharist* (Wilmington, Delaware, = patristic anthology).

3. Mediaeval

J. de Montclos, *Lanfranc et Bérenger* (Louvain 1971).

J. Geiselmann, *Die Abendmahlslehre an der Wende der christlichen Spätantike zum Frühmittelalter* (Munich 1933).
Idem, *Die Eucharistielehre der Vorscholastik* (Paderborn 1926).
G. Macy, *The Theologies of the Eucharist in the Early Scholastic Period* (Oxford 1985).
B. Neunheuser, *Eucharistie in Mittelalter und Neuzeit* (Freiburg 1967).
C. E. Sheedy, *The Eucharistic Controversy of the Eleventh Century* (Washington 1947).

For St Thomas, see:
W. Barden, *Saint Thomas Aquinas, Summa Theologiae Vol. 58, The Eucharistic Presence* (London 1965).
T. Gilby, *Saint Thomas Aquinas, Summa Theologiae, Vol. 59, Holy Communion* (London 1975).

4. Reformation and Trent
F. Clark, *The Eucharistic Sacrifice and the Reformation* (London 1960).
L. Godefroy, 'Eucharistie d'aprés le concile de Trente', *Dictionnaire de Théologie Catholique* V. 2 (1913; 1924), cols. 1326–1356.
G. Kelly, 'Eucharistic Sacrifice at Trent', *Irish Theological Quarterly* 51, 4 (1985), pp. 268–288.
D. N. Power, *The Sacrifice We Offer. The Tridentine Dogma and its Re-Interpretation* (Edinburgh 1987).
J. Riviére, 'La Messe durant la période de la Réforme et du concile de Trente', *Dictionnaire de Théologie Catholique* X. 1 (Paris 1928), cols. 1085–1142.

5. The early modern period
E. Hocedez, *Histoire de la Théologie au 19e siècle*, III (Brussels 1947), pp. 280–306.
E. Mangenot, 'Eucharistie, du 16e au 20e siècle', *Dictionnaire de Théologie Catholique* V.2 (Paris 1919), cols. 1356–1368.
A. Michel, 'La Messe chez les théologiens postérieurs au concile de Trente. Essence et efficacité', ibid., X. 1 (Paris 1928), cols. 1143–1316.

C. Modern theologians:
C.B. Daly, 'Eucharistic Devotion', *Irish Theological Quarterly* 35, 4 (1968), pp. 315–342.
F. X. Durrwell, *The Eucharist: Presence of Christ* (New York 1974).
J. H. Emminghaus, *The Eucharist. Essence, Form, Celebration* (Collegeville, Minnesota, 1978).
C. V. Héris, *Le mystère de l'Eucharistie* (Paris 1943).
C. Journet, *La Messe, présence du sacrifice de la Croix* (Fribourg 1957).
N. Lash, *His Presence in the World. A Study of Eucharistic Worship and Theology* (London 1968); for criticism of this work, see B. Kelly, CSSp, 'The Eucharist: Sacrifice or Meal?', *Irish Theological Quarterly* 35, 3 (1968), pp. 298–306.
E. R. Mascall, *Corpus Christi* (London 1965; Anglican).
E. Masure, *The Sacrifice of the Mystical Body* (London 1954).
N. Mitchell, *Cult and Controversy. The Worship of the Eucharist outside Mass* (New York 1982).
M.-J. Nicolas, *What is the Eucharist?* (London 1960).
C. O'Neill, *New Approaches to the Eucharist* (Dublin 1967).

The Holy Eucharist

K.B. Osborne, 'Contemporary Understandings of the Eucharist: A Survey of Catholic Thinking', *Journal of Ecumenical Studies* 13 (1976), pp. 192-213.

J. Powers, *Eucharistic Theology* (London 1967).

K. Rahner and A. Häussling, *The Celebration of the Eucharist* (London 1968).

A.M. Roguet, *Holy Mass. Appraoches to the Mystery* (London 1953).

E. Schillebeeckx, *The Eucharist* (London 1968).

M. de la Taille, *The Mystery of Faith* (London 1941-50).

A. Vonier, *A Key to the Doctrine of the Eucharist* (London 1946).

D. Appendix on Anglicanism

W. R. Crockett, 'Holy Communion', in S. Sykes and J. Booty (eds.), The *Study of Anglicanism* (London 1988), pp. 272-285.

C. W. Dugmore, *Eucharistic Doctrine in England from Hooker to Waterland* (London 1942).

A. Härderlin, *The Tractarian Understanding of the Eucharist* (Uppsala 1965).

E. R. Mascall, et al., *A Critique of Eucharistic Agreement* (London 1975).

J. E. Rattenbury, *The Eucharistic Hymns of John and Charles Wesley* (London 1948).

For the agreed statement of ARCIC I on the Eucharist:

Anglican-Roman Catholic International Commission, *The Final Report* (London 1982).

Index of Names

A

Abraham 14
Adamantios 40
Afanas'ev, N. 107
Alexander II, Pope 63
Althusser, A. 117
Amalarius of Metz 74
Ambrose 49, 63, 80
Ambrosius Catherinus 91
Aquinas: see Thomas Aquinas
Athanasius 37–38
Athenagoras 46
Augustine 40, 42, 49, 50–55, 56,
  62, 64, 74, 80, 83, 85, 87

B

Balthasar, H.U. von 120–122
Barrett, C.K. 9
Bellarmine, Robert 94
Berengar 62–65, 68, 74, 114
Biel, Gabriel 89–91
Bouyer, L. 107
Brown, R. 10
Bultmann, R. 9

C

Cano, Melchior 93
Catherine of Siena 120
Chadwick, H. 64
Charles the Bald 60
Clark F. 91
Clement of Alexandria 34
Congar, Y. 107
Cornelius a Lapide 32
Cranmer, T. 125
Cullmann, O. 9
Cyprian 37, 48, 49
Cyril of Alexandria 45–46, 47
Cyril of Jerusalem 38–39, 44

D

De Condren, C. 97–99

De la Taille, M. 40, 102–104
De Lubac, H. 83, 107
De Montcheuil, Y. 113
Dix, G. 39

E

Edward VI 125, 127
Ephraem Syrus 103
Epiphanius, deacon 41
Epiphanius of Salamis 23
Eusebius of Caesarea 99
Evdokimov, P. 107

F

Florus of Lyons 83
Florovsky, G. 107

G

Gelasius, Pope 43
Gerhoh of Reichersberg 84
Gilbert de la Porrée 83, 84
Gregory VII, Pope 64, 67
Gregory of Elvira 83
Gregory Nazianzen 50, 95
Gregory of Nyssa 42, 44, 45
Grisewood, H. 105
Gutiérrez, G. 117–118

H

Hanson, R.P.C. 131–132
Harnack, A. von 35
Hedley, J.C. 94–95
Hildebrand, see Gregory VII, Pope
Honorius of Autun 77
Hooker, R. 125
Humbert of Silva Candida 62, 67

I

Ignatius of Antioch 36
Ildephonsus of Toledo 83
Innocent III, Pope 66, 67

Irenaeus 36, 47–48, 56
Isidore of Seville 83

J

James II 127
Jeremias, J. 21
Jerome 56
John, evangelist 9–19, 21–22, 63
John Paul II, Pope 122–123
John Chrysostom 44, 49, 50, 54, 118
John Damascene 42
Jonas of Orleans 83
Jones, D. 102, 104–105
Judas Iscariot 16, 17, 20
Justin 36, 46, 47, 48

K

Kilmartin, E. 118

L

Lanfranc 63, 68
Lanne, E. 107
Leenhardt, F. 112
Leo the Great, Pope 38
Leo IX, Pope 62
Leonard, G. 130
Leys, L. 94
Loisy, A. 17, 33
Lugo, John de 94
Luke, evangelist 16, 27, 32–33
Luther, M. 65, 89

M

Macarius of Magnesia 40
Macy, G. 84
Marcellus of Ancyra 99
Mark, evangelist 16, 19, 22, 23, 27
Mary I 125
Mary II 127
Matthew, evangelist 16, 19, 22, 27, 28, 117
Meehan, F. X. 119
Meyendorff, J. 107
Michael Kerullarios 62
Moses 13, 27

N

Nestorius 46
Newman, J.H. 33
Nicholas II, Pope 62

O

Olier, J.J. 97–98
O'Neill, C. 109–111
Origen 34, 49

P

Paschasius Radbert 59–60
Paul, apostle 19, 27, 29–32, 35, 86
Paul VI, Pope 110, 116, 122
Perrone, G. 94
Peter, apostle 12
Peter Abelard 84
Peter Lombard 85, 88
Pighius, A. 91
Pius VI, Pope 100
Pius XII, Pope 108, 110
Power, D. 92
Pseudo-Thomas 91

R

Rahner, K. 107–111
Ratramnus 60–61, 65
Ratzinger, J. 107
Rupert of Deutz 77

S

Salmeron, A. 94
Saward, J. 120
Scheeben, M.J. 95–96
Schillebeeckx, E. 111
Serapion 49
Smits, L. 113
Stone, D. 42, 66
Suárez, F. 94

T

Tertullian 34, 35, 37, 46
Thalhofer, V. 96–97
Theodoret 43, 54
Thomas Aquinas 30, 50, 58, 67–74,
76, 77–78, 79–83

V

Vásquez, G. 94
Victorinus of Petau 23
Vonier, A. 40, 102

W

Wainwright, G. 56
Walafrid Strabo 83
Waterland, D. 128
Wesley, C. 127
Wesley, J. 127
William of Auxerre 80
William III 127

Z

Zizioulas, J. 107
Zwingli, H. 65